A CHOICE OF
BLAKE'S VERSE

A CHOICE OF BLAKE'S VERSE

selected

with an introduction by

KATHLEEN RAINE

FABER AND FABER

3 Queen Square

London

First published in 1970
by Faber and Faber Limited
3 Queen Square London W.C.1
Reprinted 1972
Printed in Great Britain
by R. MacLehose and Company Limited
The University Press Glasgow
All rights reserved
Introduction © Kathleen Raine 1970

ISBN 0 571 09268 3 (paper edition)
ISBN 0 571 09241 1 (hard cover edition)

Contents

6

9

"There is No Natural Religion"
"All Religions are One"
"Annotations to Lavater's Aphorisms on Man"
"Annotations to Swedenborg's Wisdom of the Angels

On Reserve.

The text of the poems in this volume is taken from *The Complete Writings of William Blake* edited by Geoffrey Keynes (Oxford University Press).

Introduction

William Blake (1757-1827) was born in London, the son of a hosier in Golden Square. But for four years at Felpham on the South Coast near Worthing, his whole life was lived in his native city.

Blake's education was that of an artist and craftsman; as a boy he attended Pars' drawing-school, and was afterwards apprenticed to the engraver Basire, under whose signature a number of Blake's prentice works appeared. Once, for a short time, assisted by his beloved younger brother Robert and his wife Catherine, he set up his own print-shop, but this was a financial failure. Blake's originality was too extreme for the fashion of his time, and his more ambitious ventures, his illustrations to Blair's *The Grave* and to Young's *Night Thoughts,* brought him little success. But he was never without work; at best for such fine books as Erasmus Darwin's *Botanic Garden;* at worst, he engraved soup-tureens and the like for the Wedgwood catalogues. Only towards the end of his life, through the practical help of Linnell, then a young artist, and the admiring encouragement of a group (which included Samuel Palmer, Finch, Calvert and George Richmond) for whom Blake was 'the Interpreter', was he able to devote himself to his greatest works, the Job engravings and unfinished series of illustrations to Dante.

As a painter he found few patrons; his one exhibition passed all but unnoticed. His poems likewise were too out of the ordinary for his age, and only his first volume of verse, his juvenilia, *Poetical Sketches,* was published in book form. But Blake's misfortune is our good fortune; for, failing to find any other publisher, he became his own. His wonderful illuminated books, in whose pages words and designs each enhance the other's meaning and beauty, can be compared only with illuminated psalters of that mediaeval 'Gothic' art he admired.

Blake is the supreme poet of his native city, though not in a descriptive sense. There are a few depictions, in the background of his designs, of the Gothic towers of Westminster, symbol of the true spiritual Christianity; and of Wren's St. Paul's, which represented, for him, 'natural religion'. Those roseate cloudscapes and golden sunbursts which in luminosity resemble those of another Londoner, Blake's younger contemporary Turner, may yet be seen in all their beauty over Hampstead and Battersea. But for Blake the city is above all the sum of the human experience it embodies; it is the expression of man. Blake is an artist of the human form, a poet of the human experience. His city is the 'fourfold London' of the mind, heart, senses and imagination, sum of the thoughts and feelings, the splendours and miseries of its people. 'I behold London, a Human awful wonder of God!', he wrote,

My streets are my Ideas of Imagination
. . . .
My houses are Thoughts, my Inhabitants, Affections,
The children of my thoughts walking within my blood-vessels.

Like all cities, London is at any time the embodiment of the spiritual state of its inhabitants, for better or for worse, 'ever consuming & ever building'.

The actors in Blake's human drama are not individuals but 'states' of the human soul, collectivities, group-souls. 'Man Passes on, but States remain for Ever'. 'It ought to be understood that the Persons, Moses and Abraham, are not here meant, but the States Signified by those Names. . . when distant they appear as One Man, but as you approach they appear multitudes of Nations.' These collectivities he derived in part from the teaching of his early master Swedenborg; from whom he also took the term 'the Divine Humanity', the collective being of all those 'in Christ'; Blake's 'Jesus the Imagination' is not so much an individual as a kingdom:

Then those in Great Eternity met in the Council of God
As one man, for contracting their Exalted Senses
They behold Multitude or Expanding they behold as one.
As One Man all the Universal family . . .

12

Blake called himself a prophet; for him poetry was the inspired voice of the imagination, the divine in man. He placed himself (as did also the English poet closest to him, Milton), in the Jewish prophetic tradition, because the Jews put their faith rather in inspiration than (as did the Greek philosophers) in reason:

'We of Israel taught that the Poetic Genius (as you now call it) was the first principle and all others merely derivative, which was the cause of our despising the priests and philosophers of other countries, and prophecying that all Gods would at last be proved to originate in ours & to be the tributaries of the Poetic Genius.

All religions, he believed, are one; ' The religions of all Nations are derived from each Nation's different reception of the Poetic Genius, which is everywhere call'd the Spirit of Prophecy. . . the True Man is the Source, he being the Poetic Genius.'

His belief that 'All deities reside in the human breast' notwithstanding, Blake was not in the current sense of the word a humanist; for him man was, above all, a 'form and organ' of the divine life. Because Blake denounced social injustice, and because he was an enthusiast for the American Revolution and a friend of Paine, he is often claimed by the political left of the present time. Far from being a forerunner of those atheist materialist ideologies which in our own society have attained such power and prestige, he waged against materialism his lifelong mental fight. 'Bacon, Locke and Newton, are the three great teachers of atheism, or Satan's doctrine,' he told Crabb Robinson the diarist. The Industrial Revolution he saw as an expression of the mechanistic philosophy represented, for him, by these three names. Blake's 'Satanic Mills' were not only or primarily those factories which in his day had scarcely begun to create their appalling and inhuman landscape, but the mechanistic philosophy of which these are an expression. He records the sufferings of the enslaved, the labourers in the brick-kilns and mills, of chimney-sweepers, prostitutes, soldiers. But man's enslavement, as Blake saw it, results precisely from those materialist ideologies, both in England and in France, of which Marxism is the ultimate triumph. For Blake the only true liberty is the spiritual freedom offered by Christianity; the enslavement of modern man is due precisely to those ideologies of which the Industrial Revolution is the direct consequence. A younger generation in total revolt against the premises of a technological Utopia turn naturally to William Blake for a coherent and militant alternative.

He criticized the Christian Churches of his day for 'deism', which he regarded as a capitulation to atheist science. 'There is,' he said, 'no natural religion;' for 'Every natural effect has a spiritual cause and not a natural. Natural cause only seems.' To Christianity Blake gave a modern relevence whose range and depth we are only beginning to discover; but in doing so he made no kind of compromise with scientific theory. A 'demythologised' Christianity had no part in his new vision; he restored, on the contrary, to demythologized Protestant England a pantheon of living gods, the Four Zoas and their feminine 'emanations', the soul-figure Jerusalem and the cruel 'Goddess Nature', Vala. Those archetypal beings seem less strange to a generation familiarized by Jung with the idea of a 'collective' unconscious peopled by such figures as Blake depicted and described, than to those matter-of-fact minds of the nineteenth century who thought him an inspired madman. Those abiding inhabitants of 'the human breast' he clothed in forms and attributes appropriate to the industrial age: Los with his printing-press and his 'furnaces'; Enitharmon with her 'looms'; purblind, rational Urizen with his pen and spectacles; Orc, spirit of revolution, with his 'wine-press' of war.

The Last Judgement, so central a theme in Blake's prophetic poems *Vala* or *The Four Zoas,* and *Jerusalem,* signifies, for him, the triumph of the Imagination over false ideologies:

Some people flatter themselves that there will be no Last Judgment, & that Bad Art will be adopted & mixed with Good Art, That Error or Experiment will make a part of Truth & they Boast that it is its Foundation. These People flatter themselves: I will not flatter them. Error is Created. Truth is Eternal.

Blake's Jerusalem, City of God, is not to be attained by altering external conditions which make men not better but only 'better off'; but by changing man himself, through an awakening from the 'deadly sleep' of unconsciousness. If man changes, his world will change; for we build our cities in the image of our dreams.

The imaginative vision signifies the attainment of full human consciousness. This, as Blake understood, cannot come about through rational discursive thought: 'Reason, or the ratio of all we have already known, is not the same that it shall be when we know more.' For 'Man by his reasoning power can only compare & judge of what he has already perceiv'd.' It is by a cleansing of the 'doors of perception', the senses, the 'chief inlets of Soul in this age' that new knowledge comes. Aldous Huxley has borrowed the phrase as the title of a book on the effects of a 'psychedelic' drug; but Blake knew that the imaginative vision was not to be had at so cheap a rate; for him it was the labour of a lifetime:

> . . . I rest not from my great task
> To open the Eternal Worlds, to open the Immortal Eyes
> Of man inwards into Worlds of Thought, into Eternity,
> Ever expanding in the Bosom of God, the Human Imagination.

Our world is what we perceive; and we perceive, for the most part, imperfectly and falsely; 'error, or creation,' Blake says, 'is Burnt up the Moment Men cease to behold it.' Blake wrote in a letter to an employer:

I feel that man may be happy In This World, And I know that This World Is a World of Imagination & Vision. I see Every thing I paint In This World, but Every body does not see alike. To the Eyes of a Miser a Guinea is more beautiful than the sun, & a bag worn with the use of money has more beautiful proportions than a Vine filled with Grapes. The tree which moves some to tears of joy is in the eyes of others only a Green thing that stands in the way. Some See Nature all Ridicule & Deformity, & by these I shall not regulate my proportions; & Some Scarce see Nature at all. But to the Eyes of the Man of Imagination, Nature is Imagination itself. As a man is, So he Sees. As the Eye is formed, such are its powers.

In the transformation of man and his world by the power of the imagination, the arts are paramount; 'Poetry, Painting & Music, the three Powers in Man of conversing with Paradise.' Jesus being the Imagination itself, his disciples were 'all artists' because they lived and acted 'from impulse, not from rules'.

I know of no other Christianity and of no other Gospel than the liberty both of body & mind to exercise the Divine Arts of Imagination; Imagination the real & eternal World of which this Vegetable Universe is but a faint shadow. . . to Labour in Knowledge is to build up Jerusalem, and to Despise Knowledge is to Despise Jerusalem & her Builders.

When Blake speaks of 'knowledge' he means spiritual knowledge; in contrast with the 'vegetable ratio' of the five senses. 'He who sees the infinite in all things, sees God. He who sees the Ratio only, sees himself only.' At the present time 'knowledge', in popular thought, is identified with science. Blake knew that the inner universe of consciousness has its laws, no less objective and no less binding than 'the laws of nature'; a truth of which modern psychology is becoming aware. What, to Blake's earliest readers, appeared to be, at best, 'originality' and at worst eccentricity and madness, proves, on the contrary, to be the language of traditional orthodoxy, spoken with prophetic eloquence to the deaf ears of a sick society. Blake's philosophy was not of his own invention; he was widely and deeply read in the literature of the Perennial Philosophy. His chosen masters were Swedenborg and the German mystical theologian, Jacob Boehme; he was familiar with Plotinus and the Neoplatonists, and also with Plato himself, through the writings and translations of Thomas Taylor 'the English Pagan', a member of his own London circle. He knew something of Hindu, Norse and Celtic mythology, the Hermetica, Christian Cabbala, and the literature of Alchemy. No less familiar was he with the writings of his ideological enemies, Bacon, Newton and Locke, Rousseau and Voltaire; as is shown by the attention he gave to their arguments and the penetration with which he refutes them. His sensitive engraver's finger was at all times on the living pulse of his age.

'The Sickness of Albion' which Blake so searchingly diagnosed and so laboured to cure has, in our century, reached a crisis which may prove fatal; but just possibly a new generation, repudiating the materialist values of a technological Utopia, may listen to William Blake, who saw, foresaw, and prescribed the only cure for the ills of our society.

Blake's themes of childhood reflect an interest much 'in the air' at the end of the eighteenth century, both in England and in France. The hymn-writer Watts's *Divine Songs for Children* and more especially his *Moral Songs* are echoed, and often contradicted, in Blake's *Songs of Innocence and Experience*. Rousseau, whose ideas were to revolutionize education, had an active follower in England in Blake's friend Mary Wollstonecraft; Blake illustrated her own book for children *Original Stories from Real Life*; and his *Songs of Innocence* are his own contribution to what was at the time a new form of writing. His book of emblems, *The Gates of Paradise*, was first designed 'for Children'; many years later he republished these emblems with the Prologue, 'keys' and Epilogue here given, under the new title, 'For the Sexes'. The poem *Tiriel* is written upon the theme of repressive education and parental tyranny; and the much finer *Visions of the Daughters of Albion* contains many of Mary Wollstonecraft's ideas (taken from Rousseau) both on education and on the freedom of sexual love. Blake differs from Rousseau, however, in claiming this freedom not for the once-born natural man but only for the 'divine humanity', twice-born into the kingdom of 'Jesus the Imagination'.

It was Blake's way to express insights, states of mind, or 'ideologies' in terms of the kind of being to whom they belong. If this principle were to be put into practice it might often save us from being fooled by the specious talk of persons whom, as human beings, we could never for a moment respect for their qualities of wisdom or goodness. Such a being is Tiriel, and so is short-sighted Urizen, 'Aged Ignorance', the tyrant rationalism.

Most of the passages from the Prophetic Books are spoken by the *personae* of Blake's gods, or inhabitants, as he says, of 'the human breast'. It is not only or principally what is said, but who among our moods is the speaker, that matters: Jesus the Imagination or Satan the Selfhood, or passionate Orc, cold rational Urizen, or some other. A brief outline of Blake's pantheon may serve as a guide:

Blake's drama of Man's Fall, Judgment and Redemption takes place within the collective being of the human race, 'the eternal man'; or, more specifically, of the English nation, 'the Giant Albion'. Within Man two kingdoms are in conflict: 'Satan the

Selfhood', or, as modern psychologists would say, the human ego, the Kingdom cut off from the God Within; who is 'Jesus the Imagination, the indwelling divine principle, Lord of the "Kingdom not of this world", "Eden, the land of life." ' The soul-figure (Jung's *anima*,) takes several forms — as Thel, Oothoon, and Vala — before she takes her final personification as Jerusalem, bride of Jesus. Vala (who in the earlier books is both the higher and the lower aspect of the soul) is, in *Jerusalem*, only the soul's 'shadow', 'the Shadowy Female', the goddess Nature whose 'cruelty' seeks to seduce man's love and draw it down into the 'world of generation'.

There are, as in Jungian psychology, four 'Zoas', or functions of humanity. The name is taken from the 'living creatures' of Ezekiel's vision; not could any psychologist better Blake's definition of them:

Four Mighty Ones are in every Man; a Perfect Unity Cannot Exist but from the Universal Brotherhood of Eden, The Universal Man, to Whom be Glory Evermore. Amen. What are the Natures of those Living Creatures the Heav'nly Father only Knoweth. No Individual knoweth nor can know in all Eternity.

The four are Urizen (reason) Luvah (love) Tharmas (sensual life) and (Los) visionary intuition. Each has an unfallen and a fallen or temporal aspect, or 'spectre'; in several instances the Spectral form is differently named, as Orc, the fallen aspect of Love, revolutionary violence and warlike passion. Each Zoa has a feminine 'vehicle' or 'emanation': Ahania, wife of Urizen; Vala of Luvah; Enion (matter) of Tharmas, and Enitharmon, the embodier of his 'visions', wife of Los. Each Zoa has also his 'sons' and 'daughters', natural principles (as the Fates are 'daughters' of Urizen) or human beings, as the poets are 'sons' of Los.

In the drama of Albion's Fall, Blake assigns the greatest blame to rationalism - Urizen - and to the 'goddess Nature' of whom Albion is enamoured. In the redemptive process, the major role is assigned to Los, 'the eternal Prophet', inspirer of poetry and the other arts, who 'kept the Divine Vision in time of trouble'. Blake tells in an inspired passage in *Milton* how he himself became possessed by that great daemon in whose 'furnaces of affliction' the redemption of Albion is, in process of time, to be accomplished.

Blake's *Songs of Innoncence and Experience* are known to all. Those who think of him as an inspired and childlike visionary are commonly dismayed and astonished at a first encounter with Blake's great Prophetic Books, *Milton* and *Jerusalem;* whose frequent obscurity is illumined by lightning-flashes of clarity; and through whose phantasmagoria gods and daemons float, as W. B. Yeats, their first editor and commentator says, 'muttering wisdom'. But there was only one William Blake; the depth and force of meaning of the Prophetic Books is to be found also in the *Songs;* and the purity and visionary light and joy of *Songs of Innocence,* no less than the burning sombre splendour of *Songs of Experience,* illuminates many of the most beautiful passages of *Milton.* Seen in the light of his total achievement our one national prophet emerges as a greater figure; whether we approach him as the prophet of the Industrial Revolution; as the reasoned opponent of the materialist philosophers; the predecessor of modern psychology, or the herald of a New Age; or, more simply, as the finest master of the metrics of the long line in English poetry.

KATHLEEN RAINE

From *Poetical Sketches*

SONG

How sweet I roam'd from field to field,
   And tasted all the summer's pride,
'Till I the prince of love beheld,
   Who in the sunny beams did glide!

He shew'd me lilies for my hair,
   And blushing roses for my brow;
He led me through his gardens fair,
   Where all his golden pleasures grow.

With sweet May dews my wings were wet,
   And Phœbus fir'd my vocal rage;
He caught me in his silken net,
   And shut me in his golden cage.

He loves to sit and hear me sing,
   Then, laughing, sports and plays with me;
Then strerches out my golden wing,
   And mocks my loss of liberty.

SONG

My silks and fine array,
   My smiles and languish'd air,
By love are driv'n away;
   And mournful lean Despair
Brings me yew to deck my grave:
Such end true lovers have.

His face is fair as heav'n,
  When springing buds unfold;
O why to him was't giv'n,
  Whose heart is wintry cold?
His breast is love's all worship'd tomb,
Where all love's pilgrims come.

Bring me an axe and spade,
  Bring me a winding sheet;
When I my grave have made,
  Let winds and tempests beat:
Then down I'll lie, as cold as clay.
True love doth pass away!

TO THE MUSES

Whether on Ida's shady brow,
  Or in the chambers of the East,
The chambers of the sun, that now
  From antient melody have ceas'd;

Whether in Heav'n ye wander fair,
  Or the green corners of the earth,
Or the blue regions of the air,
  Where the melodious winds have birth;

Whether on chrystal rocks ye rove,
  Beneath the bosom of the sea
Wand'ring in many a coral grove,
  Fair Nine, forsaking Poetry!

How have you left the antient love
  That bards of old enjoy'd in you!
The languid strings do scarcely move!
  The sound is forc'd, the notes are few!

From *The Marriage of Heaven and Hell*

A MEMORABLE FANCY

How do you know but ev'ry Bird that cuts the airy way,
Is an immense world of delight, clos'd by your senses five?

Poems from Blake's Note-books

Never pain to tell thy love
Love that never told can be;
For the gentle wind does move
Silently, invisibly.

I told my love, I told my love,
I told her all my heart,
Trembling, cold, in ghastly fears—
Ah, she doth depart.

Soon as she was gone from me
A traveller came by
Silently, invisibly—
O, was no deny.

If you trap the moment before it's ripe,
The tears of repentance you'll certainly wipe;
But if once you let the ripe moment go
You can never wipe off the tears of woe.

Mock on, Mock on, Voltaire, Rousseau:
Mock on, Mock on: 'tis all in vain!
You throw the sand against the wind,
And the wind blows it back again.

And every sand becomes a Gem
Reflected in the beams divine;
Blown back they blind the mocking Eye,
But still in Israel's paths they shine.

The Atoms of Democritus
And Newton's Particles of light
Are sands upon the Red sea shore,
Where Israel's tents do shine so bright.

SEVERAL QUESTIONS ANSWERED

What is it men in women do require?
The lineaments of Gratified Desire.
What is it women do in men require?
The lineaments of Gratified Desire.

*

He who binds to himself a joy
Doth the winged life destroy;
But he who kisses the joy as it flies
Lives in Eternity's sun rise.

*

The look of love alarms
Because 'tis fill'd with fire;
But the look of soft deceit
Shall Win the lover's hire.

*

Soft deceit & Idleness,
These are Beauty's sweetest dress.

*

An ancient Proverb:
Remove away that black'ning church,
Remove away that marriage hearse,
Remove away that — of blood,
You'll quite remove the ancient curse.

He.   Where thou dwellest, in what Grove
      Tell me, Fair one, tell me, love;
      Where thou thy charming Nest dost build,
      O thou pride of every field!

She.   Yonder stands a lonely tree,
      There I live & mourn for thee.
      Morning drinks my silent tear,
      And evening winds my sorrows bear.

He.   O thou Summer's harmony,
      I have liv'd & mourn'd for thee.
      Each day I mourn along the wood,
      And night hath heard my sorrows loud.

She.   Dost thou truly long for me?
      And am I thus sweet to thee?
      Sorrow now is at an End,
      O my Lover & my Friend!

He.   Come, on wings of joy we'll fly
      To where my Bower hangs on high!
      Come, & make thy calm retreat
      Among green leaves & blossoms sweet!

THE MENTAL TRAVELLER

I travel'd thro' a Land of Men,
A Land of Men & Women too,
And heard & saw such dreadful things
As cold Earth wanderers never knew.

For there the Babe is born in joy
That was begotten in dire woe;
Just as we Reap in joy the fruit
Which we in bitter tears did sow.

And if the Babe is born a Boy
He's given to a Woman Old,
Who nails him down upon a rock,
Catches his shrieks in cups of gold.

She binds iron thorns around his head,
She pierces both his hands & feet,
She cuts his heart out at his side
To make it feel both cold & heat.

Her fingers number every Nerve,
Just as a Miser counts his gold;
She lives upon his shrieks & cries,
And she grows young as he grows old.

Till he becomes a bleeding youth,
And she becomes a Virgin bright;
Then he rends up his Manacles
And binds her down for his delight.

He plants himself in all her Nerves,
Just as a Husbandman his mould;
And she becomes his dwelling place
And Garden fruitful seventy fold.

An aged Shadow, soon he fades,
Wand'ring round an Earthly Cot,
Full filled all with gems & gold
Which he by industry had got.

And these are the gems of the Human Soul,
The rubies & pearls of a lovesick eye,
The countless gold of the akeing heart,
The martyr's groan & the lover's sigh.

They are his meat, they are his drink;
He feeds the Beggar & the Poor
And the wayfaring Traveller:
For ever open is his door.

His grief is their eternal joy;
They make the roofs & walls to ring;
Till from the fire on the hearth
A little Female Babe does spring.

And she is all of solid fire
And gems & gold, that none his hand
Dares stretch to touch her Baby form,
Or wrap her in his swaddling-band.

But She comes to the Man she loves,
If young or old, or rich or poor;
They soon drive out the aged Host,
A Beggar at another's door.

He wanders weeping far away,
Until some other take him in;
Oft blind & age-bent, sore distrest,
Until he can a Maiden win.

And to allay his freezing Age
The Poor Man takes her in his arms;
The Cottage fades before his sight,
The Garden & its lovely Charms.

The Guests are scatter'd thro' the land
For the Eye altering alters all;
The Senses roll themselves in fear,
And the flat Earth becomes a Ball;

The stars, sun, Moon, all shrink away,
A desart vast without a bound,
And nothing left to eat or drink,
And a dark desart all around.

The honey of her Infant lips,
The bread & wine of her sweet smile,
The wild game of her roving Eye,
Does him to Infancy beguile;

For as he eats & drinks he grows
Younger & younger every day;
And on the desart wild they both
Wander in terror & dismay.

Like the wild Stag she flees away,
Her fear plants many a thicket wild;
While he pursues her night & day,
By various arts of Love beguil'd,

By various arts of Love & Hate,
Till the wide desart planted o'er
With Labyrinths of wayward Love,
Where roam the Lion, Wolf & Boar,

Till he becomes a wayward Babe,
And she a weeping Woman Old.
Then many a Lover wanders here;
The Sun & Stars are nearer roll'd.

The trees bring forth sweet Extacy
To all who in the desart roam;
Till many a City there is Built,
And many a pleasant Shepherd's home.

But when they find the frowning Babe,
Terror strikes thro' the region wide:
They cry "The Babe! the Babe is Born!"
And flee away on Every side.

For who dare touch the frowning form,
His arm is wither'd to its root;
Lions, Boars, Wolves, all howling flee,
And every Tree does shed its fruit.

And none can touch that frowning form,
Except it be a Woman Old;
She nails him down upon the Rock,
And all is done as I have told.

THE LAND OF DREAMS

Awake, awake, my little Boy!
Thou wast thy Mother's only joy;
Why dost thou weep in thy gentle sleep?
Awake! thy Father does thee keep.

"O, what Land is the Land of Dreams?
"What are its Mountains & what are its Streams?
"O Father, I saw my Mother there,
"Among the Lillies by waters fair.

"Among the Lambs, clothed in white,
"She walk'd with her Thomas in sweet delight.
"I wept for joy, like a dove I mourn;
"O! when shall I again return?"

Dear Child, I also by pleasant Streams
Have wander'd all Night in the Land of Dreams;
But tho' calm & warm the waters wide,
I could not get to the other side.

"Father, O Father! what do we here
"In this Land of unbelief & fear?
"The Land of Dreams is better far,
"Above the light of the Morning Star."

★

I rose up at the dawn of day—
Get thee away! get thee away!
Pray'st thou for Riches? away! away!
This is the Throne of Mammon grey.

Said I, "this sure is very odd.
"I took it to be the Throne of God.
"For every Thing besides I have:
"It is only for Riches that I can crave.

"I have Mental Joy & Mental Health
"And Mental Friends & Mental wealth;
"I've a Wife I love & that loves me;
"I've all But Riches Bodily.

"I am in God's presence night & day,
"And he never turns his face away.
"The accuser of sins by my side does stand
"And he holds my money bag in his hand.

"For my worldly things God makes him pay,
"And he'd pay for more if to him I would pray;
"And so you may do the worst you can do:
"Be assur'd Mr devil I won't pray to you.

"Then If for Riches I must not Pray,
"God knows I little of Prayers need say.
"So as a Church is known by its Steeple,
"If I pray it must be for other People.

"He says, if I do not worship him for a God,
"I shall eat coarser food & go worse shod;
"So as I don't value such things as these,
"You must do, Mr devil, just as God please."

THE CRYSTAL CABINET

The Maiden caught me in the Wild,
Where I was dancing merrily;
She put me into her Cabinet
And Lock'd me up with a golden Key.

This Cabinet is form'd of Gold
And Pearl & Crystal shining bright,
And within it opens into a World
And a little lovely Moony Night.

Another England there I saw,
Another London with its Tower,
Another Thames & other Hills,
And another pleasant Surrey Bower,

Another Maiden like herself,
Translucent, lovely, shining clear,
Threefold each in the other clos'd—
O, what a pleasant trembling fear!

O, what a smile; a threefold Smile
Fill'd me, that like a flame I burn'd;
I bent to Kiss the lovely Maid,
And found a Threefold Kiss return'd.

I strove to sieze the inmost Form
With ardor fierce & hands of flame,
But burst the Crystal Cabinet,
And like a Weeping Babe became—

A weeping Babe upon the wild,
And Weeping Woman pale reclin'd,
And in the outward air again
I fill'd with woes the passing Wind.

AUGURIES OF INNOCENCE

To see a World in a Grain of Sand
And a Heaven in a Wild Flower,
Hold Infinity in the palm of your hand
And Eternity in an hour.

A Robin Red breast in a Cage
Puts all Heaven in a Rage.
A dove house fill'd with doves & Pigeons
Shudders Hell thro' all its regions.
A dog starv'd at his Master's Gate
Predicts the ruin of the State.
A Horse misus'd upon the Road
Calls to Heaven for Human blood.
Each outcry of the hunted Hare
A fibre from the Brain does tear.
A Skylark wounded in the wing,
A Cherubim does cease to sing.
The Game Cock clip'd & arm'd for fight
Does the Rising Sun affright.
Every Wolf's & Lion's howl
Raises from Hell a Human Soul.
The wild deer, wand'ring here & there,
Keeps the Human Soul from Care.
The Lamb misus'd breeds Public strife
And yet forgives the Butcher's Knife.
The Bat that flits at close of Eve
Has left the Brain that won't Believe.
The Owl that calls upon the Night
Speaks the Unbeliever's fright.
He who shall hurt the little Wren
Shall never be belov'd by Men.
He who the Ox to wrath has mov'd
Shall never be by Woman lov'd.
The wanton Boy that kills the Fly
Shall feel the Spider's enmity.
He who torments the Chafer's sprite
Weaves a Bower in endless Night.
The Catterpiller on the Leaf
Repeats to thee thy Mother's grief.
Kill not the Moth nor Butterfly,
For the Last Judgment draweth nigh.
He who shall train the Horse to War
Shall never pass the Polar Bar.

The Begger's Dog & Widow's Cat,
Feed them & thou wilt grow fat.
The Gnat that sings his Summer's song
Poison gets from Slander's tongue.
The poison of the Snake & Newt
Is the sweat of Envy's Foot.
The Poison of the Honey Bee
Is the Artist's Jealousy.
The Prince's Robes & Beggar's Rags
Are Toadstools on the Miser's Bags.
A truth that's told with bad intent
Beats all the Lies you can invent.
It is right it should be so;
Man was made for Joy & Woe;
And when this we rightly know
Thro' the World we safely go.
Joy & Woe are woven fine,
A Clothing for the Soul divine
Under every grief & pine
Runs a joy with silken twine.
The Babe is more than swadling Bands;
Throughout all these Human Lands
Tools were made, & Born were hands,
Every Farmer Understands.
Every Tear from Every Eye
Becomes a Babe in Eternity;
This is caught by Females bright
And return'd to its own delight.
The Bleat, the Bark, Bellow & Roar
Are Waves that Beat on Heaven's Shore.
The Babe that weeps the Rod beneath
Writes Revenge in realms of death.
The Beggar's Rags, fluttering in Air,
Does to Rags the Heavens tear.
The Soldier, arm'd with Sword & Gun,
Palsied strikes the Summer's Sun.
The poor Man's Farthing is worth more
Than all the Gold on Afric's Shore.

One Mite wrung from the Labrer's hands
Shall buy & sell the Miser's Lands:
Or, if protected from on high,
Does that whole Nation sell & buy.
He who mocks the Infant's Faith
Shall be mock'd in Age & Death.
He who shall teach the Child to Doubt
The rotting Grave shall ne'er get out.
He who respects the Infant's faith
Triumphs over Hell & Death.
The Child's Toys & the Old Man's Reasons
Are the Fruits of the Two seasons.
The Questioner, who sits so sly,
Shall never know how to reply.
He who replies to words of Doubt
Doth put the Light of Knowledge out.
The Strongest Poison ever known
Came from Caesar's Laurel Crown.
Nought can deform the Human Race
Like to the Armour's iron brace.
When Gold & Gems adorn the Plow
To peaceful Arts shall Envy Bow.
A Riddle or the Cricket's Cry
Is to Doubt a fit Reply.
The Emmet's Inch & Eagle's Mile
Make Lame Philosophy to smile.
He who Doubts from what he sees
Will ne'er Believe, do what you Please.
If the Sun & Moon should doubt,
They'd immediately Go out.
To be in a Passion you Good may do,
But no Good if a Passion is in you.
The Whore & Gambler, by the State
Licenc'd, build that Nation's Fate.
The Harlot's cry from Street to Street
Shall weave Old England's winding Sheet.
The Winner's Shout, the Loser's Curse,
Dance before dead England's Hearse.

Every Night & every Morn
Some to Misery are Born.
Every Morn & every Night
Some are Born to sweet delight.
Some are Born to sweet delight,
Some are Born to Endless Night.
We are led to Believe a Lie
When we see not Thro' the Eye
Which was Born in a Night to perish in a Night
When the Soul Slept in Beams of Light.
God Appears & God is Light
To those poor Souls who dwell in Night,
But does a Human Form Display
To those who Dwell in Realms of day.

Songs of Innocence

INTRODUCTION

Piping down the valleys wild,
Piping songs of pleasant glee,
On a cloud I saw a child,
And he laughing said to me:

"Pipe a song about a Lamb!"
So I piped with merry chear.
"Piper, pipe that song again;"
So I piped: he wept to hear.

"Drop thy pipe, thy happy pipe;
"Sing thy songs of happy chear:"
So I sung the same again,
While he wept with joy to hear.

"Piper, sit thee down and write
"In a book that all may read."
So he vanish'd from my sight,
And I pluck'd a hollow reed,

And I made a rural pen,
And I stain'd the water clear,
And I wrote my happy songs
Every child may joy to hear.

A DREAM

Once a dream did weave a shade
O'er my Angel-guarded bed,
That an Emmet lost its way
Where on grass methought I lay.

Troubled, 'wilder'd, and forlorn,
Dark, benighted, travel-worn,
Over many a tangled spray,
All heart-broke I heard her say:

"O, my children! do they cry?
"Do they hear their father sigh?
"Now they look abroad to see:
"Now return and weep for me."

Pitying, I drop'd a tear;
But I saw a glow-worm near,
Who replied: "What wailing wight
"Calls the watchman of the night?

"I am set to light the ground,
"While the beetle goes his round:
"Follow now the beetle's hum;
"Little wanderer, hie thee home."

36

In futurity
I prophetic see
That the earth from sleep
(Grave the sentence deep)

Shall arise and seek
For her maker meek;
And the desart wild
Become a garden mild.

In the southern clime,
Where the summer's prime
Never fades away,
Lovely Lyca lay.

Seven summers old
Lovely Lyca told;
She had wander'd long
Hearing wild birds' song.

"Sweet sleep, come to me
"Underneath this tree.
"Do father, mother weep,
"Where can Lyca sleep?

"Lost in desart wild
"Is your little child.
"How can Lyca sleep
"If her mother weep?

"If her heart does ake
"Then let Lyca wake;
"If my mother sleep,
"Lyca shall not weep.

"Frowning, frowning night,
"O'er this desart bright
"Let thy moon arise
"While I close my eyes."

Sleeping Lyca lay
While the beasts of prey,
Come from caverns deep,
View'd the maid asleep.

The kingly lion stood
And the virgin view'd,
Then he gambol'd round
O'er the hallow'd ground.

Leopards, tygers, play
Round her as she lay,
While the lion old
Bow'd his mane of gold

And her bosom lick,
And upon her neck
From his eyes of flame
Ruby tears there came;

While the lioness
Loos'd her slender dress,
And naked they convey'd
To caves the sleeping maid.

THE LITTLE GIRL FOUND

All the night in woe
Lyca's parents go
Over vallies deep,
While the desarts weep.

Tired and woe-begone,
Hoarse with making moan,
Arm in arm seven days
They trac'd the desart ways.

Seven nights they sleep
Among shadows deep,
And dream they see their child
Starv'd in desart wild.

Pale, thro' pathless ways
The fancied image strays
Famish'd, weeping, weak,
With hollow piteous shriek.

Rising from unrest,
The trembling woman prest
With feet of weary woe:
She could no further go.

In his arms he bore
Her, arm'd with sorrow sore;
Till before their way
A couching lion lay.

Turning back was vain:
Soon his heavy mane
Bore them to the ground.
Then he stalk'd around,

Smelling to his prey;
But their fears allay
When he licks their hands,
And silent by them stands.

They look upon his eyes
Fill'd with deep surprise,
And wondering behold
A Spirit arm'd in gold.

On his head a crown,
On his shoulders down
Flow'd his golden hair.
Gone was all their care.

"Follow me," he said;
"Weep not for the maid;
"In my palace deep
"Lyca lies asleep."

Then they followed
Where the vision led,
And saw their sleeping child
Among tygers wild.

To this day they dwell
In a lonely dell;
Nor fear the wolvish howl
Nor the lion's growl.

THE LAMB

Little Lamb, who made thee?
Dost thou know who made thee?
Gave thee life, & bid thee feed
By the stream & o'er the mead;
Gave thee clothing of delight,
Softest clothing, wooly, bright;
Gave thee such a tender voice,
Making all the vales rejoice?
  Little Lamb, who made thee?
  Dost thou know who made thee?

Little Lamb, I'll tell thee,
Little Lamb, I'll tell thee:
He is called by thy name,
For he calls himself a Lamb.
He is meek, & he is mild;
He became a little child.
I a child, & thou a lamb,
We are called by his name.
Little Lamb, God bless thee!
Little Lamb, God bless thee!

THE BLOSSOM

Merry, Merry Sparrow!
Under leaves so green
A happy Blossom
Sees you swift as arrow
Seek your cradle narrow
Near my Bosom.

Pretty, Pretty Robin!
Under leaves so green
A happy Blossom
Hears you sobbing, sobbing
Pretty, Pretty Robin,
Near my Bosom.

THE ECCHOING GREEN

The Sun does arise,
And make happy the skies;
The merry bells ring
To welcome the Spring;
The skylark and thrush,

The birds of the bush,
Sing louder around
To the bells' chearful sound,
While our sports shall be seen
On the Ecchoing Green.

Old John, with white hair,
Does laugh away care,
Sitting under the oak,
Among the old folk.
They laugh at our play,
And soon they all say:
"Such, such were the joys
"When we all, girls & boys,
"In our youth time were seen
"On the Ecchoing Green."

Till the little ones, weary,
No more can be merry;
The sun does descend,
And our sports have an end.
Round the laps of their mothers
Many sisters and brothers,
Like birds in their nest,
Are ready for rest,
And sport no more seen
On the darkening Green.

THE DIVINE IMAGE

To Mercy, Pity, Peace, and Love
All pray in their distress;
And to these virtues of delight
Return their thankfulness.

For Mercy, Pity, Peace, and Love
Is God, our father dear,
And Mercy, Pity, Peace, and Love
Is Man, his child and care.

For Mercy has a human heart,
Pity a human face,
And Love, the human form divine,
And Peace, the human dress.

Then every man, of every clime,
That prays in his distress,
Prays to the human form divine,
Love, Mercy, Pity, Peace.

And all must love the human form,
In heathen, turk, or jew;
Where Mercy, Love, & Pity dwell
There God is dwelling too.

THE CHIMNEY SWEEPER

When my mother died I was very young,
And my Father sold me while yet my tongue
Could scarcely cry "'weep! 'weep! 'weep! 'weep!"
So your chimneys I sweep, & in soot I sleep.

There's little Tom Dacre, who cried when his head,
That curl'd like a lamb's back, was shav'd: so I said
"Hush, Tom! never mind it, for when your head's bare
"You know that the soot cannot spoil your white hair."

And so he was quiet, & that very night
As Tom was a-sleeping, he had such a sight!
That thousands of sweepers, Dick, Joe, Ned, & Jack,
Were all of them lock'd up in coffins of black.

And by came an Angel who had a bright key,
And he open'd the coffins & set them all free;
Then down a green plain leaping, laughing, they run,
And wash in a river, and shine in the Sun.

Then naked & white, all their bags left behind,
They rise upon clouds and sport in the wind;
And the Angel told Tom, if he'd be a good boy,
He'd have God for his father, & never want joy.

And so Tom awoke; and we rose in the dark,
And got with our bags & our brushes to work.
Tho' the morning was cold, Tom was happy & warm;
So if all do their duty they need not fear harm.

INFANT JOY

"I have no name:
"I am but two days old."
What shall I call thee?
"I happy am,
"Joy is my name."
Sweet joy befall thee!

Pretty joy!
Sweet joy but two days old,
Sweet joy I call thee:
Thou dost smile,
I sing the while,
Sweet joy befall thee!

THE SHEPHERD

How sweet is the Shepherd's sweet lot!
From the morn to the evening he strays;
He shall follow his sheep all the day,
And his tongue shall be filled with praise.

For he hears the lamb's innocent call,
And he hears the ewe's tender reply;
He is watchful while they are in peace,
For they know when their Shepherd is nigh.

NIGHT

The sun descending in the west,
The evening star does shine;
The birds are silent in their nest,
And I must seek for mine.
The moon like a flower
In heaven's high bower,
With silent delight
Sits and smiles on the night.

Farewell, green fields and happy groves,
Where flocks have took delight.
Where lambs have nibbled, silent moves
The feet of angels bright;
Unseen they pour blessing
And joy without ceasing,
On each bud and blossom,
And each sleeping bosom.

They look in every thoughtless nest,
Where birds are cover'd warm;
They visit caves of every beast.
To keep them all from harm.
If they see any weeping
That should have been sleeping,
They pour sleep on their head,
And sit down by their bed.

When wolves and tygers howl for prey,
They pitying stand and weep;
Seeking to drive their thirst away,
And keep them from the sheep;
But if they rush dreadful,
The angels, most heedful,
Recieve each mild spirit,
New worlds to inherit.

And there the lion's ruddy eyes
Shall flow with tears of gold,
And pitying the tender cries,
And walking round the fold,
Saying "Wrath, by his meekness,
"And by his health, sickness
"Is driven away
"From our immortal day.

"And now beside thee, bleating lamb,
"I can lie down and sleep;
"Or think on him who bore thy name,
"Graze after thee and weep.
"For, wash'd in life's river,
"My bright mane for ever
"Shall shine like the gold
"As I guard o'er the fold."

A CRADLE SONG

Sweet dreams, form a shade
O'er my lovely infant's head;
Sweet dreams of pleasant streams
By happy, silent, moony beams.

Sweet sleep, with soft down
Weave thy brows an infant crown.
Sweet sleep, Angel mild,
Hover o'er my happy child.

Sweet smiles, in the night
Hover over my delight;
Sweet smiles, Mother's smiles,
All the livelong night beguiles.

Sweet moans, dovelike sighs,
Chase not slumber from thy eyes.
Sweet moans, sweeter smiles,
All the dovelike moans beguiles.

Sleep, sleep, happy child,
All creation slept and smil'd;
Sleep, sleep, happy sleep,
While o'er thee thy mother weep.

Sweet babe, in thy face
Holy image I can trace.
Sweet babe, once like thee,
Thy maker lay and wept for me,

Wept for me, for thee, for all,
When he was an infant small.
Thou his image ever see,
Heavenly face that smiles on thee,

Smiles on thee, on me, on all;
Who became an infant small.
Infant smiles are his own smiles;
Heaven & earth to peace beguiles.

THE LITTLE BOY LOST

"Father! father! where are you going?
"O do not walk so fast.
"Speak, father, speak to your little boy,
"Or else I shall be lost."

The night was dark, no father was there;
The child was wet with dew;
The mire was deep, & the child did weep,
And away the vapour flew.

THE LITTLE BOY FOUND

The little boy lost in the lonely fen,
Led by the wand'ring light,
Began to cry; but God, ever nigh,
Appear'd like his father in white.

He kissed the child & by the hand led
And to his mother brought,
Who in sorrow pale, thro' the lonely dale,
Her little boy weeping sought.

NURSE'S SONG

When the voices of children are heard on the green
And laughing is heard on the hill,
My heart is at rest within my breast
   And everything else is still.

"Then come home, my children, the sun is gone down
"And the dews of night arise;
"Come, come, leave off play, and let us away
"Till the morning appears in the skies."

"No , no, let us play, for it is yet day
"And we cannot go to sleep;
"Besides, in the sky the little birds fly
"And the hills are all cover'd with sheep."

"Well, well, go & play till the light fades away
"And then go home to bed."
The little ones leaped & shouted & laugh'd
   And all the hills ecchoed.

HOLY THURSDAY

'Twas on a Holy Thursday, their innocent faces clean,
The children walking two & two, in red & blue & green,
Grey-headed beadles walk'd before, with wands as white as snow
Till into the high dome of Paul's they like Thames' waters flow.

O what a multitude they seem'd, these flowers of London town !
Seated in companies they sit with radiance all their own.
The hum of multitudes was there, but multitudes of lambs,
Thousands of little boys & girls raising their innocent hands.

Now like a mighty wind they raise to heaven the voice of song,
Or like harmonious thunderings the seats of heaven among.
Beneath them sit the aged men, wise guardians of the poor;
Then cherish pity, lest you drive an angel from your door.

ON ANOTHER'S SORROW

Can I see another's woe,
And not be in sorrow too?
Can I see another's grief,
And not seek for kind relief?

Can I see a falling tear,
And not feel my sorrow's share?
Can a father see his child
Weep, nor be with sorrow fill'd?

Can a mother sit and hear
An infant groan, an infant fear?
No, no! never can it be!
Never, never can it be!

And can he who smiles on all
Hear the wren with sorrows small,
Hear the small bird's grief & care,
Hear the woes that infants bear,

And not sit beside the nest,
Pouring pity in their breast;
And not sit the cradle near,
Weeping tear on infant's tear;

And not sit both night & day,
Wiping all our tears away?
O! no never can it be!
Never, never can it be!

He doth give his joy to all;
He becomes an infant small;
He becomes a man of woe;
He doth feel the sorrow too.

Think not thou canst sigh a sigh
And thy maker is not by;
Think not thou canst weep a tear
And thy maker is not near.

O! he gives to us his joy
That our grief he may destroy;
Till our grief is fled & gone
He doth sit by us and moan.

SPRING

Sound the Flute!
Now it's mute.
Birds delight
Day and Night;
Nightingale
In the Dale,
Lark in Sky,
Merrily,
Merrily, Merrily, to welcome in the Year.

Little Boy,
Full of joy;
Little Girl,
Sweet and small;
Cock does crow,
So do you;
Merry voice,
Infant noise,
Merrily, Merrily, to welcome in the Year.

Little Lamb,
Here I am;
Come and lick
My white neck;
Let me pull
Your soft Wool;
Ler me kiss
Your soft face:
Merrily, Merrily, we welcome in the Year.

THE SCHOOL BOY

I love to rise in a summer morn
When the birds sing on every tree;
The distant huntsman winds his horn,
And the sky-lark sings with me.
O! what sweet company.

But to go to school in a summer morn,
O! it drives all joy away;
Under a cruel eye outworn,
The little ones spend the day
In sighing and dismay.

Ah! then at times I drooping sit,
And spend many an anxious hour,
Nor in my book can I take delight,
Nor sit in learning's bower,
Worn thro' with the dreary shower.

How can the bird that is born for joy
Sit in a cage and sing?
How can a child, when fears annoy,
But droop his tender wing,
And forget his youthful spring?

O ! father & mother if buds are nip'd
And blossoms blown away,
And if the tender plants are strip'd
Of their joy in the springing day,
By sorrow and care's dismay,

How shall the summer arise in joy,
Or the summer fruits appear?
Or how shall we gather what griefs destroy,
Or bless the mellowing year,
When the blasts of winter appear?

LAUGHING SONG

When the green woods laugh with the voice of joy,
And the dimpling stream runs laughing by;
When the air does laugh with our merry wit,
And the green hill laughs with the noise of it;

When the meadows laugh with lively green,
And the grasshopper laughs in the merry scene,
When Mary and Susan and Emily
With their sweet round mouths sing "Ha, Ha, He !"

When the painted birds laugh in the shade,
Where our table with cherries and nuts is spread,
Come live & be merry, and join with me,
To sing the sweet chorus of "Ha, Ha, He !"

THE LITTLE BLACK BOY

My mother bore me in the southern wild,
And I am black, but O ! my soul is white;
White as an angel is the English child,
But I am black, as if bereav'd of light.

53

My mother taught me underneath a tree,
And sitting down before the heat of day,
She took me on her lap and kissed me,
And pointing to the east, began to say:

"Look on the rising sun: there God does live,
"And gives his light, and gives his heat away;
"And flowers and trees and beasts and men receive
"Comfort in morning, joy in the noonday.

"And we are put on earth a little space,
"That we may learn to bear the beams of love;
"And these black bodies and this sunburnt face
"Is but a cloud, and like a shady grove.

"For when our souls have learn'd the heat to bear,
"The cloud will vanish; we shall hear his voice,
"Saying: 'Come out from the grove, my love & care,
" 'And round my golden tent like lambs rejoice.' "

Thus did my mother say, and kissed me;
And thus I say to little English boy.
When I from black and he from white cloud free,
And round the tent of God like lambs we joy,

I'll shade him from the heat, till he can bear
To lean in joy upon our father's knee;
And then I'll stand and stroke his silver hair,
And be like him, and he will then love me.

Youth of delight, come hither,
And see the opening morn,
Image of truth new born.
Doubt is fled, & clouds of reason,
Dark disputes & artful teazing.
Folly is an endless maze,
Tangled roots perplex her ways.
How many have fallen there!
They stumble all night over bones of the dead,
And feel they know not what but care,
And wish to lead others, when they should be led.

Songs of Experience

INTRODUCTION

Hear the voice of the Bard!
Who Present, Past, & Future, sees;
Whose ears have heard
The Holy Word
That walk'd among the ancient trees,

Calling the lapsed Soul,
And weeping in the evening dew;
That might controll
The starry pole,
And fallen, fallen light renew!

"O Earth, O Earth, return!
"Arise from out the dewy grass;
"Night is worn,
"And the morn
"Rises from the slumberous mass.

"Turn away no more;
"Why wilt thou turn away?
"The starry floor,
"The wat'ry shore,
"Is giv'n thee till the break of day."

EARTH'S ANSWER

Earth rais'd up her head
From the darkness dread & drear.
Her light fled,
Stony dread!
And her locks cover'd with grey despair.

"Prison'd on wat'ry shore,
"Starry Jealousy does keep my den:
"Cold and hoar,
"Weeping o'er,
"I hear the Father of the ancient men.

"Selfish father of men!
"Cruel, jealous, selfish fear!
"Can delight,
"Chain'd in night,
"The virgins of youth and morning bear?

"Does spring hide its joy
"When buds and blossoms grow?
"Does the sower
"Sow by night,
"Or the plowman in the darkness plow?

"Break this heavy chain
"That does freeze my bones around.
"Selfish! vain!
"Eternal bane!
"That free Love with bondage bound."

THE CLOD & THE PEBBLE

"Love seeketh not Itself to please,
"Nor for itself hath any care,
"But for another gives its ease,
"And builds a Heaven in Hell's despair."

So sang a little Clod of Clay
Trodden with the cattle's feet,
But a Pebble of the brook
Warbled out these metres meet:

"Love seeketh only Self to please,
"To bind another to Its delight,
"Joys in another's loss of ease,
"And builds a Hell in Heaven's despite."

HOLY THURSDAY

Is this holy thing to see
In a rich and fruitful land,
Babes reduc'd to misery,
Fed with cold and usurous hand?

Is that trembling cry a song?
Can it be a song of joy?
And so many children poor?
It is a land of poverty!

And their sun does never shine,
And their fields are bleak & bare,
And their ways are fill'd with thorns:
It is eternal winter there.

For where-e'er the sun does shine,
And where-e'er the rain does fall,
Babe can never hunger there,
Nor poverty the mind appall.

THE CHIMNEY SWEEPER

A little black thing among the snow,
Crying ' 'weep ! 'weep !' in notes of woe !
"Where are thy father & mother? say?"
"They are both gone up to the church to pray.

"Because I was happy upon the heath,
"And smil'd among the winter's snow,
"They clothed me in the clothes of death,
"And taught me to sing the notes of woe.

"And because I am happy & dance & sing,
"They think they have done me no injury,
"And are gone to praise God & his Priest & King,
"Who make up a heaven of our misery."

NURSE'S SONG

When the voices of children are heard on the green
And whisp'rings are in the dale,
The days of my youth rise fresh in my mind,
My face turns green and pale.

Then come home, my children, the sun is gone down,
And the dews of night arise;
Your spring & your day are wasted in play,
And your winter and night in disguise.

THE SICK ROSE

O Rose, thou art sick!
The invisible worm
That flies in the night,
In the howling storm,

Has found out thy bed
Of crimson joy:
And his dark secret love
Does thy life destroy.

THE FLY

Little Fly,
Thy summer's play
My thoughtless hand
Has brush'd away.

Am not I
A fly like thee?
Or art not thou
A man like me?

For I dance,
And drink, & sing,
Till some blind hand
Shall brush my wing.

If thought is life
And strength & breath,
And the want
Of thought is death;

Then am I
A happy fly,
If I live
Or if I die.

THE ANGEL

I Dreamt a Dream ! what can it mean?
And that I was a maiden Queen,
Guarded by an Angel mild;
Witless woe was ne'er beguil'd !

And I wept both night and day,
And he wip'd my tears away,
And I wept both day and night,
And hid from him my heart's delight.

So he took his wings and fled;
Then the morn blush'd rosy red;
I dried my tears, & arm'd my fears
With ten thousand shields and spears.

Soon my Angel came again:
I was arm'd, he came in vain;
For the time of youth was fled,
And grey hairs were on my head.

THE TYGER

Tyger ! Tyger ! burning bright
In the forests of the night,
What immortal hand or eye
Could frame thy fearful symmetry?

In what distant deeps or skies
Burnt the fire of thine eyes?
On what wings dare he aspire?
What the hand dare sieze the fire?

And what shoulder, & what art,
Could twist the sinews of thy heart?
And when thy heart began to beat,
What dread hand? & what dread feet?

What the hammer? what the chain?
In what furnace was thy brain?
What the anvil? what dread grasp
Dare its deadly terrors clasp?

When the stars threw down their spears,
And water'd heaven with their tears,
Did he smile his work to see?
Did he who made the Lamb make thee?

Tyger! Tyger! burning bright
In the forests of the night,
What immortal hand or eye
Dare frame thy fearful symmetry?

MY PRETTY ROSE TREE

A flower was offer'd to me,
Such a flower as May never bore;
But I said "I've a Pretty Rose-tree,"
And I passed the sweet flower o'er.

Then I went to my Pretty Rose-tree,
To tend her by day and by night;
But my Rose turn'd away with jealousy,
And her thorns were my only delight.

AH! SUN-FLOWER

Ah, Sun-flower, weary of time,
Who countest the steps of the Sun,
Seeking after that sweet golden clime
Where the traveller's journey is done:

Where the Youth pined away with desire,
And the pale Virgin shrouded in snow
Arise from their graves, and aspire
Where my Sun-flower wishes to go.

THE LILLY

The modest Rose puts forth a thorn,
The humble Sheep a threat'ning horn;
While the Lilly white shall in Love delight,
Nor a thorn, nor a threat, stain her beauty bright.

THE GARDEN OF LOVE

I went to the Garden of Love,
And saw what I never had seen:
A Chapel was built in the midst,
Where I used to play on the green.

And the gates of this Chapel were shut,
And "Thou shalt not" writ over the door;
So I turn'd to the Garden of Love
That so many sweet flowers bore;

And I saw it was filled with graves,
And tomb-stones where flowers should be;
And Priests in black gowns were walking their rounds,
And binding with briars my joys & desires.

THE LITTLE VAGABOND

Dear Mother, dear Mother, the Church is cold,
But the Ale-house is healthy & pleasant & warm;
Besides I can tell where I am used well,
Such usage in heaven will never do well.

But if at the Church they would give us some Ale,
And a pleasant fire our souls to regale,
We'd sing and we'd pray all the live-long day,
Nor ever once wish from the Church to stray.

Then the Parson might preach, & drink, & sing,
And we'd be as happy as birds in the spring;
And modest dame Lurch, who is always at Church,
Would not have bandy children, nor fasting, nor birch.

And God, like a father rejoicing to see
His children as pleasant and happy as he,
Would have no more quarrel with the Devil or the Barrel,
But kiss him, & give him both drink and apparel.

LONDON

I wander thro' each charter'd street,
Near where the charter'd Thames does flow,
And mark in every face I meet
Marks of weakness, marks of woe.

In every cry of every Man,
In every Infant's cry of fear,
In every voice, in every ban,
The mind-forg'd manacles I hear.

How the Chimney-sweeper's cry
Every black'ning Church appalls;
And the hapless Soldiers sigh
Runs in blood down Palace walls.

But most thro' midnight streets I hear
How the youthful Harlot's curse
Blasts the new born Infant's tear,
And blights with plagues the Marriage hearse.

THE HUMAN ABSTRACT

Pity would be no more
If we did not make somebody Poor;
And Mercy no more could be
If all were as happy as we.

And mutual fear brings peace,
Till the selfish loves increase:
Then Cruelty knits a snare,
And spreads his baits with care.

He sits down with holy fears,
And waters the ground with tears;
Then Humility takes its root
Underneath his foot.

Soon spreads the dismal shade
Of Mystery over his head;
And the Catterpiller and Fly
Feed on the Mystery.

And it bears the fruit of Deceit,
Ruddy and sweet to eat;
And the Raven his nest has made
In its thickest shade.

The Gods of the earth and sea
Sought thro' Nature to find this Tree;
But their search was all in vain:
There grows one in the Human Brain.

INFANT SORROW

My mother groan'd! my father wept.
Into the dangerous world I leapt:
Helpless, naked, piping loud:
Like a fiend hid in a cloud.

Struggling in my father's hands,
Striving against my swadling bands,
Bound and weary I thought best
To sulk upon my mother's breast.

A POISON TREE

I was angry with my friend:
I told my wrath, my wrath did end.
I was angry with my foe:
I told it not, my wrath did grow.

And I water'd it in fears,
Night & morning with my tears;
And I sunned it with smiles,
And with soft deceitful wiles.

And it grew both day and night,
Till it bore an apple bright;
And my foe beheld it shine,
And he knew that it was mine,

And into my garden stole
When the night had veil'd the pole:
In the morning glad I see
My foe outstretch'd beneath the tree.

A LITTLE BOY LOST

"Nought loves another as itself,
"Nor venerates another so,
"Nor is it possible to Thought
"A greater than itself to know:

"And Father, how can I love you
"Or any of my brothers more?
"I love you like the little bird
"That picks up crumbs around the door."

The Priest sat by and heard the child,
In trembling zeal he siez'd his hair:
He led him by his little coat,
And all admir'd the Priestly care.

And standing on the altar high,
"Lo! what a fiend is here!" said he,
"One who sets reason up for judge
"Of our most holy Mystery."

The weeping child could not be heard,
The weeping parents wept in vain;
They strip'd him to his little shirt,
And bound him in an iron chain;

And burn'd him in a holy place,
Where many had been burn'd before:
The weeping parents wept in vain.
Are such things done on Albion's shore?

A LITTLE GIRL LOST

Children of the future Age
Reading this indignant page,
Know that in a former time
Love! sweet Love! was thought a crime.

In the Age of Gold,
Free from winter's cold,
Youth and maiden bright
To the holy light,
Naked in the sunny beams delight.

Once a youthful pair,
Fill'd with softest care,
Met in garden bright
Where the holy light
Had just remov'd the curtains of the night

There, in rising day
On the grass they play;
Parents were afar,
Strangers came not near,
And the maiden soon forgot her fear.

Tired with kisses sweet,
They agree to meet
When the silent sleep
Waves o'er heaven's deep,
And the weary tired wanderers weep.

To her father white
Came the maiden bright;
But his loving look,
Like the holy book,
All her tender limbs with terror shook.

"Ona! pale and weak!
"To thy father speak:
"O, the trembling fear!
"O, the dismal care!
"That shakes the blossoms of my hoary hair."

TO TIRZAH

Whate'er is Born of Mortal Birth
Must be consumed with the Earth
To rise from Generation free:
Then what have I to do with thee?

The Sexes sprung from Shame & Pride,
Blow'd in the morn; in evening died;
But Mercy chang'd Death into Sleep;
The Sexes rose to work & weep.

Thou, Mother of my Mortal part,
With cruelty didst mould my Heart,
And with false self-decieving tears
Didst bind my Nostrils, Eyes, & Ears:

Didst close my Tongue in sensless clay,
And me to Mortal Life betray.
The Death of Jesus set me free:
Then what have I to do with thee?

68

A DIVINE IMAGE

Etched about 1794, but not included by Blake

Cruelty has a Human Heart,
And Jealousy a Human Face;
Terror the Human Form Divine,
And Secrecy the Human Dress.

The Human Dress is forged Iron,
The Human Form a fiery Forge,
The Human Face a Furnace seal'd,
The Human Heart its hungry Gorge.

From *Tiriel*

TIRIEL'S CURSE

"Why is one law given to the lion & the patient Ox?
"Dost thou not see that men cannot be formed all alike,
"Some nostril'd wide, breathing out blood. Some close shut up
"In silent deceit, poisons inhaling from the morning rose,
"With daggers hid beneath their lips & poison in their tongue;
"Or eyed with little sparks of Hell, or with infernal brands
"Flinging flames of discontent & plagues of dark despair;
"Or those whose mouths are graves, whose teeth the gates of eternal
    death.
"Can wisdom be put in a silver rod, or love in a golden bowl?
"Is the son of a king warmed without wool? or does he cry with a
    voice
"Of thunder? does he look upon the sun & laugh or stretch
"His little hands into the depths of the sea, to bring forth
"The deadly cunning of the scaly flatterer & spread it to the
    morning?

"And why men bound beneath the heavens in a reptile form,
"A worm of sixty winters creeping on the dusky ground?
"The child springs from the womb; the father ready stands to form
"The infant head, while the mother idle plays with her dog on her
    couch:
"The young bosom is cold for lack of mother's nourishment, &
    milk
"Is cut off from the weeping mouth: with difficulty & pain
"The little lids are lifted & the little nostrils open'd:
"The father forms a whip to rouze the sluggish senses to act
"And scourges off all youthful fancies from the new-born man.
"Then walks the weak infant in sorrow, compell'd to number foot-
    steps
"Upon the sand.
"And when the drone has reach'd his crawling length,
"Black berries appear that poison all around him. Such was Tiriel,
"Compell'd to pray repugnant & to humble the immortal spirit
"Till I am subtil as a serpent in a paradise,
"Consuming all, both flowers & fruits, insects & warbling birds.
"And now my paradise is fall'n & a drear sandy plain
"Returns my thirsty hissings in a curse on thee, O Har,
"Mistaken father of a lawless race, my voice is past."

From *Visions of the Daughters of Albion*

THE WOES OF OOTHOON

"With what sense is it that the chicken shuns the ravenous hawk?
"With what sense does the tame pigeon measure out the expanse?
"With what sense does the bee form cells? have not the mouse &
    frog
"Eyes and ears and sense of touch? yet are their habitations
"And their pursuits as different as their forms and as their joys.
"Ask the wild ass why he refuses burdens, and the meek camel
"Why he loves man: is it because of eye, ear, mouth, or skin,
"Or breathing nostrils? No, for these the wolf and tyger have.
"Ask the blind worm the secrets of the grave, and why her spires
"Love to curl round the bones of death; and ask the rav'nous snake

70

"Where she gets poison, & the wing'd eagle why he loves the sun;
"And then tell me the thoughts of man, that have been hid of old.

*

"O Urizen! Creator of men! mistaken Demon of heaven!
"Thy joys are tears, thy labour vain to form men to thine image.
"How can one joy absorb another? are not different joys
"Holy, eternal, infinite? and each joy is a Love.

"Does not the great mouth laugh at a gift, & the narrow eyelids
    mock
"At the labour that is above payment? and wilt thou take the ape
"For thy councellor, or the dog for a schoolmaster to thy children?
"Does he who contemns poverty and he who turns with abhorrence
"From usury feel the same passion, or are they moved alike?
"How can the giver of gifts experience the delights of the merchant?
"How the industrious citizen the pains of the husbandman?
"How different far the fat fed hireling with hollow drum,
"Who buys whole corn fields into wastes, and sings upon the heath!
"How different their eye and ear! how different the world to them!
"With what sense does the parson claim the labour of the farmer?
"What are his nets & gins & traps; & how does he surround him
"With cold floods of abstraction, and with forests of solitude,
"To build him castles and high spires, where kings & priests may
    dwell;
"Till she who burns with youth, and knows no fixed lot, is bound
"In spells of law to one she loathes? and must she drag the chain
"Of life in weary lust? must chilling, murderous thoughts obscure
"The clear heaven of her eternal spring; to bear the wintry rage
"Of a harsh terror, driv'n to madness, bound to hold a rod
"Over her shrinking shoulders all the day, & all the night
"To turn the wheel of false desire, and longings that wake her
    womb
"To the abhorred birth of cherubs in the human form,
"That live a pestilence & die a meteor, & are no more;
"Till the child dwell with one he hates, and do the deed he loaths,
"And the impure scourge force his seed into its unripe birth
"Ere yet his eyelids can behold the arrows of the day?

71

"Does the whale worship at thy footsteps as the hungry dog;
"Or does he scent the mountain prey because his nostrils wide
"Draw in the ocean? does his eye discern the flying cloud
"As the raven's eye? or does he measure the expanse like the
        vulture?
"Does the still spider view the cliffs where eagles hide their young;
"Or does the fly rejoice because the harvest is brought in?
"Does not the eagle scorn the earth & despise the treasures beneath?
"But the mole knoweth what is there, & the worm shall tell it thee.
"Does not the worm erect a pillar in the mouldering church yard
"And a palace of eternity in the jaws of the hungry grave?
"Over his porch these words are written: 'Take thy bliss, O Man!
" 'And sweet shall be thy taste, & sweet thy infant joys renew!'
"Infancy! fearless, lustful, happy, nestling for delight
"In laps of pleasure: Innocence! honest, open, seeking
"The vigorous joys of morning light; open to virgin bliss.
"Who taught thee modesty, subtil modesty, child of night & sleep?
"When thou awakest wilt thou dissemble all thy secret joys,
"Or wert thou not awake when all this mystery was disclos'd?
"Then com'st thou forth a modest virgin, knowing to dissemble,
"With nets found under thy night pillow, to catch virgin joy
"And brand it with the name of whore, & sell it in the night,
"In silence, ev'n without a whisper, and in seeming sleep.
"Religious dreams and holy vespers light thy smoky fires:
"Once were thy fires lighted by the eyes of honest morn.
"And does my Theotormon seek this hypocrite modesty,
"This knowing, artful, secret, fearful, cautious, trembling hypocrite
"Then is Oothoon a whore indeed! and all the virgin joys
"Of life are harlots, and Theotormon is a sick man's dream;
"And Oothoon is the crafty slave of selfish holiness.

"But Oothoon is not so: a virgin fill'd with virgin fancies,
"Open to joy and to delight where ever beauty appears;
"If in the morning sun I find it, there my eyes are fix'd
"In happy copulation; if in evening mild, wearied with work,
"Sit on a bank and draw the pleasures of this free born joy.

"The moment of desire! the moment of desire! The virgin
"That pines for man shall awaken her womb to enormous joys

72

"In the secret shadows of her chamber: the youth shut up from
"The lustful joy shall forget to generate & create an amorous image
"In the shadows of his curtains and in the folds of his silent pillow.
"Are not these the places of religion, the rewards of continence,
"The self enjoyings of self denial? why dost thou seek religion?
"Is it because acts are not lovely that thou seekest solitude
"Where the horrible darkness is impressed with reflections of desire?

"Father of Jealousy, be thou accursed from the earth!
"Why hast thou taught my Theotormon this accursed thing?
"Till beauty fades from off my shoulders, darken'd and cast out,
"A solitary shadow wailing on the margin of non-entity.

"I cry: Love! Love! Love! happy happy Love! free as the moun-
    tain wind!
"Can that be Love that drinks another as a sponge drinks water,
"That clouds with jealousy his nights, with weepings all the day,
"To spin a web of age around him, grey and hoary, dark,
"Till his eyes sicken at the fruit that hangs before his sight?
"Such is self-love that envies all, a creeping skeleton
"With lamplike eyes watching around the frozen marriage bed.

"But silken nets and traps of adamant will Oothoon spread,
"And catch for thee girls of mild silver, or of furious gold.
"I'll lie beside thee on a bank & view their wanton play
"In lovely copulation, bliss on bliss, with Theotormon:
"Red as the rosy morning, lustful as the first born beam,
"Oothoon shall view his dear delight, nor e'er with jealous cloud
"Come in the heaven of generous love, nor selfish blightings bring.

"Does the sun walk in glorious raiment on the secret floor
"Where the cold miser spreads his gold; or does the bright cloud
    drop
"On his stone threshold? does his eye behold the beam that brings
"Expansion to the eye of pity? or will he bind himself
"Beside the ox to thy hard furrow? does not that mild beam blot
"The bat, the owl, the glowing tyger, and the king of night?
"The sea fowl takes the wintry blast for a cov'ring to her limbs,
"And the wild snake the pestilence to adorn him with gems & gold;

"And trees & birds & beasts & men behold their eternal joy.
"Arise, you little glancing wings, and sing your infant joy!
"Arise, and drink your bliss, for every thing that lives is holy!"

Thus every morning wails Oothoon; but Theotormon sits
Upon the margin'd ocean conversing with shadows dire.

The Daughters of Albion hear her woes, & eccho back her sighs.

The End

The Book of Thel

THEL'S MOTTO.

Does the Eagle know what is in the pit?
Or wilt thou go ask the Mole?
Can Wisdom be put in a silver rod?
Or Love in a golden bowl?

I

The daughters of Mne Seraphim led round their sunny flocks,
All but the youngest: she in paleness sought the secret air,
To fade away like morning beauty from her mortal day:
Down by the river of Adona her soft voice is heard,
And thus her gentle lamentation falls like morning dew:

"O life of this our spring! why fades the lotus of the water,
"Why fade these children of the spring, born but to smile & all?
"Ah! Thel is like a wat'ry bow, and like a parting cloud;
"Like a reflection in a glass; like shadows in the water;
"Like dreams of infants, like a smile upon an infant's face;
"Like the dove's voice; like transient day; like music in the fari.
"Ah! gentle may I lay me down, and gentle rest my head,
"And gentle sleep the sleep of death, and gentle hear the voice
"Of him that walketh in the garden in the evening time."

The Lilly of the valley, breathing in the humble grass,
Answer'd the lovely maid and said: "I am a wat'ry weed,
"And I am very small and love to dwell in lowly vales;
"So weak, the gilded butterfly scarce perches on my head.
"Yet I am visited from heaven, and he that smiles on all
"Walks in the valley and each morn over me spreads his hand,
"Saying, 'Rejoice, thou humble grass, thou new-born lilly flower,
" 'Thou gentle maid of silent valleys and of modest brooks;
" 'For thou shalt be clothed in light, and fed with morning manna,
" 'Till summer's heat melts thee beside the fountains and the springs
" 'To flourish in eternal vales.' Then why should Thel complain?

"Why should the mistress of the vales of Har utter a sigh?"

She ceas'd & smil'd in tears, then sat down in her silver shrine.

Thel answer'd: "O thou little virgin of the peaceful valley,
"Giving to those that cannot crave, the voiceless, the o'ertired;
"Thy breath doth nourish the innocent lamb, he smells thy milky
        garments,
"He crops thy flowers while thou sittest smiling in his face,
"Wiping his mild and meekin mouth from all contagious taints.
"Thy wine doth purify the golden honey; thy perfume,
"Which thou dost scatter on every little blade of grass that springs,
"Revives the milked cow, & tames the fire-breathing steed.
"But Thel is like a faint cloud kindled at the rising sun:
"I vanish from my pearly throne, and who shall find my place?"

"Queen of the vales," the Lilly answer'd, "ask the tender cloud,
"And it shall tell thee why it glitters in the morning sky,
"And why it scatters its bright beauty thro' the humid air,
"Descend, O little Cloud, & hover before the eyes of Thel."

The Cloud descended, and the Lilly bow'd her modest head
And went to mind her numerous charge among the verdant grass.

II
"O little Cloud," the virgin said, "I charge thee tell to me
"Why thou complainest not when in one hour thou fade away:

"Then we shall seek thee, but not find. Ah! Thel is like to thee:
"I pass away: yet I complain, and no one hears my voice."

The Cloud then shew'd his golden head & his bright form emerg'd
Hovering and glittering on the air before the face of Thel.

"O virgin, know'st thou not our steeds drink of the golden springs
"Where Luvah doth renew his horses? Look'st thou on my youth,
"And fearest thou, because I vanish and am seen no more,
"Nothing remains? O maid, I tell thee, when I pass away
"It is to tenfold life, to love, to peace and raptures holy:
"Unseen descending, weigh my light wings upon balmy flowers,
"And court the fair-eyed dew to take me to her shining tent:
"The weeping virgin, trembling kneels before the risen sun,
"Till we arise link'd in a golden band and never part,
"But walk united, bearing food to all our tender flowers."
    "Dost thou, O little Cloud? I fear that I am not like thee,
"For I walk thro' the vales of Har, and smell the sweetest flowers,
"But I feed not the little flowers; I hear the warbling birds,
"But I feed not the warbling birds; they fly and seek their food:
"But Thel delights in these no more, because I fade away;
"And all shall say, 'Without a use this shining woman liv'd,
"'Or did she only live to be at death the food of worms?'"

The Cloud reclin'd upon his airy throne and answer'd thus:

"Then if thou art the food of worms, O virgin of the skies,
"How great thy use, how great thy blessing! Every thing that lives
"Lives not alone nor for itself. Fear not, and I will call
"The weak worm from its lowly bed, and thou shalt hear its voice.
"Come forth, worm of the silent valley, to thy pensive queen."

The helpless worm arose, and sat upon the Lilly's leaf,
And the bright Cloud sail'd on, to find his partner in the vale.

III

Then Thel astonish'd view'd the Worm upon its dewy bed.
"Art thou a Worm? Image of weakness, art thou but a Worm?

76

"I see thee like an infant wrapped in the Lilly's leaf.
"Ah! weep not, little voice, thou canst not speak, but thou canst weep.
"Is this a Worm? I see thee lay helpless & naked, weeping,
"And none to answer, none to cherish thee with mother's smiles."

The Clod of Clay heard the Worm's voice & rais'd her pitying head:
She bow'd over the weeping infant, and her life exhal'd
In milky fondness: then on Thel she fix'd her humble eyes.

"O beauty of the vales of Har! we live not for our ourselves.
"Thou seest me the meanest thing, and so I am indeed.
"My bosom of itself is cold, and of itself is dark;
"But he, that loves the lowly, pours his oil upon my head,
"And kisses me, and binds his nuptial bands around my breast,
"And says: 'Thou mother of my children, I have loved thee
"'And I have given thee a crown that none can take away.'
"But how this is, sweet maid, I know not, and I cannot know;
"I ponder, and I cannot ponder; yet I live and love."

The daughter of beauty wip'd her pitying tears with her white veil,
And said: "Alas! I knew not this, and therefore did I weep.
"That God would love a Worm I knew, and punish the evil foot
"That wilful bruis'd its helpless form; but that he cherish'd it
"With milk and oil I never knew, and therefore did I weep;
"And I complain'd in the mild air, because I fade away,
"And lay me down in thy cold bed, and leave my shining lot."

"Queen of the vales," the matron Clay answer'd, "I heard thy sighs,
"And all thy moans flew o'er my roof, but I have call'd them down.
"Wilt thou, O Queen, enter my house? 'Tis given thee to enter
"And to return: fear nothing, enter with thy virgin feet."

IV

The eternal gates' terrific porter lifted the northern bar:
Thel enter'd in & saw the secrets of the land unknown.
She saw the couches of the dead, & where the fibrous roots
Of every heart on earth infixes deep its restless twists:
A land of sorrows & of tears where never smile was seen.

77

She wander'd in the land of clouds thro' valleys dark, list'ning
Dolours & lamentations; waiting oft beside a dewy grave
She stood in silence, list'ning to the voices of the ground,
Till to her own grave plot she came, & there she sat down,
And heard this voice of sorrow breathed from the hollow pit

"Why cannot the Ear be closed to its own destruction?
"Or the glist'ning Eye to the poison of a smile?
"Why are Eyelids stor'd with arrows ready drawn,
"Where a thousand fighting men in ambush lie?
"Or an Eye of gifts & graces show'ring fruits & coined gold?
"Why a Tongue impress'd with honey from every wind?
"Why an Ear, a whirlpool fierce to draw creations in?
"Why a Nostril wide inhaling terror, trembling, & affright?
"Why a tender curb upon the youthful burning boy?
"Why a little curtain of flesh on the bed of our desire?"

The Virgin started from her seat, & with a shriek
Fled back unhinder'd till she came into the vales of Har.

From *Europe*

A PROPHECY

"Five windows light the cavern'd Man: thro' one he breathes the air;
"Thro' one hears music of the spheres, thro' one the eternal vine
"Flourishes, that he may receive the grapes; thro' one can look
"And see small portions of the eternal world that ever groweth;
"Thro' one himself pass out what time he please; but he will not,
"For stolen joys are sweet & bread eaten in secret pleasant."

So sang a Fairy, mocking, as he sat on a streak'd Tulip,
Thinking none saw him: when he ceas'd I started from the trees
And caught him in my hat, as boys knock down a butterfly.
"How know you this," said I, "small Sir? where did you learn this
    song?"

Seeing himself in my possession, thus he answer'd me:
"My master, I am yours! command me, for I must obey."

"Then tell me, what is the material world, and is it dead?"
He, laughing, answer'd: "I will write a book on leaves of flowers,
"If you will feed me on love-thoughts & give me now and then
"A cup of sparkling poetic fancies; so, when I am tipsie,
"I'll sing to you to this soft lute, and shew you all alive
"The world, where every particle of dust breathes forth its joy."

I took him home in my warm bosom: as we went along
Wild flowers I gather'd, & he shew'd me each eternal flower:
He laugh'd aloud to see them whimper because they were pluck'd.
They hover'd round me like a cloud of incense: when I came
Into my parlour and sat down and took my pen to write,
My Fairy sat upon the table and dictated EUROPE.

PRELUDIUM

The nameless shadowy female rose from out the breast of Orc,
Her snaky hair brandishing in the winds of Enitharmon;
And thus her voice arose:

"O mother Enitharmon, wilt thou bring forth other sons?
"To cause my name to vanish, that my place may not yet be found,
"For I am faint with travel,[1]
"Like the dark cloud disburden'd in the day of dismal thunder.

"My roots are brandish'd in the heavens, my fruits in earth beneath
"Surge, foam and labour into life, first born & first consum'd!
"Consumed and consuming!
"Then why shouldst thou, accursed mother, bring me into life?

"I wrap my turban of thick clouds around my lab'ring head,
"And fold the sheety waters as a mantle round my limbs;
"Yet the red sun and moon
"And all the overflowing stars rain down prolific pains.

[1] *Probably an error for* travail.

"Unwilling I look up to heaven, unwilling count the stars:
"Sitting in fathomless abyss of my immortal shrine
"I sieze their burning power
"And bring forth howling terrors, all devouring fiery kings,

"Devouring & devoured, roaming on dark and desolate mountains,
"In forests of eternal death, shrieking in hollow trees.
"Ah mother Enitharmon!
"Stamp not with solid form this vig'rous progeny of fires.

"I bring forth from my teeming bosom myriads of flames,
"And thou dost stamp them with a signet; then they roam abroad
"And leave me void as death.
"Ah! I am drown'd in shady woe and visionary joy.

  "And who shall bind the infinite with an eternal band?
"To compass it with swaddling bands? and who shall cherish it
"With milk and honey?
"I see it smile, & I roll inward, & my voice is past."
                    She ceast, & roll'd her shady clouds
                    Into the secret place.

From *The Song of Los*

ASIA

The Kings of Asia heard
The howl rise up from Europe,
And each ran out from his Web,
From his ancient woven Den;
For the darkness of Asia was startled
At the thick-flaming, thought-creating fires of Orc.

And the Kings of Asia stood
And cried in bitterness of soul:

80

"Shall not the King call for Famine from the heath,
"Nor the Priest for Pestilence from the fen,
"To restrain, to dismay, to thin
"The inhabitants of mountain and plain,
"In the day of full-feeding prosperity
"And the night of delicious songs?

"Shall not the Councellor throw his curb
"Of Poverty on the laborius,
"To fix the price of labour,
"To invent allegoric riches?

"And the privy admonishers of men
"Call for fires in the City,
"For heaps of smoking ruins
"In the night of prosperity & wantonness?

To turn man from his path,
"To restrain the child from the womb,

"To cut off the bread from the city,
"That the remnant may learn to obey,

"That the pride of the heart may fail,
"That the lust of the eyes may be quench'd,
"That the delicate ear in its infancy
"May be dull'd, and the nostrils clos'd up,
"To teach mortal worms the path
"That leads from the gates of the Grave?"

From *The Book of Los*

Eno, aged Mother,
Who the chariot of Leutha guides
Since the day of thunders in old time,

Sitting beneath the eternal Oak
Trembled and shook the steadfast Earth,
And thus her speech broke forth:

"O Times remote!
"When Love & Joy were adoration,
"And none impure were deem'd:
"Not Eyeless Covet,
"Nor Thin-lip'd Envy,
"Nor Bristled Wrath,
"Nor Curled Wantonness;

"But Covet was poured full,
"Envy fed with fat of lambs,
"Wrath with lion's gore,
"Wantonness lull'd to sleep
"With the virgin's lute
"Or sated with her love;

"Till Covet broke his locks & bars
"And slept with open doors;
"Envy sung at the rich man's feast;
"Wrath was follow'd up and down
"By a little ewe lamb,
"And Wantonness on his own true love
"Begot a giant race."

From a letter to Thomas Butts 2 October 1800

To my Friend Butts I write
My first Vision of Light,
On the yellow sands sitting.
The Sun was Emitting
His Glorious beams
From Heaven's high Streams.
Over Sea, over Land

82

My Eyes did Expand
Into regions of air
Away from all Care,
Into regions of fire
Remote from Desire;
The Light of the Morning
Heaven's Mountains adorning:
In particles bright
The jewels of Light
Distinct shone & clear.
Amaz'd & in fear
I each particle gazed,
Astonish'd, Amazed;
For each was a Man
Human-form'd. Swift I ran,
For they beckon'd to me
Remote by the Sea,
Saying: Each grain of Sand,
Every Stone on the Land,
Each rock & each hill,
Each fountain & rill,
Each herb & each tree,
Mountain, hill, earth & sea,
Cloud, Meteor & Star,
Are Men Seen Afar.
I stood in the Streams
Of Heaven's bright beams,
And Saw Felpham sweet
Beneath my bright feet
In soft Female charms;
And in her fair arms
My Shadow I knew
And my wife's shadow too,
And My Sister & Friend.
We like Infants descend
In our Shadows on Earth,
Like a weak mortal birth.
My Eyes more & more

Like a Sea without shore
Continue Expanding,
The Heavens commanding,
Till the Jewels of Light,
Heavenly Men beaming bright,
Appear'd as One Man
Who Complacent began
My limbs to infold
In his beams of bright gold;
Like dross purg'd away
All my mire & my clay.
Soft consum'd in delight
In his bosom Sun bright
I remain'd. Soft he smil'd,
And I heard his voice Mild
Saying: This is My Fold,
O thou Ram horn'd with gold,
Who awakest from Sleep
On the Sides of the Deep.
On the Mountains around
The roarings resound
Of the lion & wolf,
The loud Sea & deep gulf.
These are guards of My Fold,
O thou Ram horn'd with gold!
And the voice faded mild.
I remain'd as a Child;
All I ever had known
Before me bright Shone.
I saw you & your wife
By the fountains of Life.
Such the Vision to me
Appear'd on the Sea.

With happiness stretch'd across the hills
In a cloud that dewy sweetness distills,
With a blue sky spread over with wings
And a mild sun that mounts & sings,
With trees & fields full of Fairy elves
And little devils who fight for themselves—
Rememb'ring the Verses that Hayley sung
When my heart knock'd against the root of my tongue—
With Angels planted in Hawthorn bowers
And God himself in the passing hours,
With Silver Angels across my way
And Golden Demons that none can stay,
With my Father hovering upon the wind
And my Brother Robert just behind
And my Brother John the evil one
In a black cloud making his mone;
Tho' dead they appear upon my path,
Notwithstanding my terrible wrath:
They beg, they intreat, they drop their tears,
Fill'd full of hopes, fill'd full of fears—
With a thousand Angels upon the Wind
Pouring disconsolate from behind
To drive them off, & before my way
A frowing Thistle implores my stay.
What to others a trifle appears
Fills me full of smiles or tears;
For double the vision my Eyes do see,
And a double vision is always with me.
With my inward Eye 'tis an old Man grey;
With my outward, a Thistle across my way.
"If thou goest back," the thistle said,
"Thou art to endless woe betray'd;
For here does Theotormon lower
And here is Enitharmon's bower

85

And Los the terrible thus hath sworn,
Because thou backward dost return,
Poverty, Envy, old age & fear
Shall bring thy Wife upon a bier;
And Butts shall give what Fuseli gave,
A dark black Rock & a gloomy Cave."

I struck the Thistle with my foot,
And broke him up from his delving root:
"Must the duties of life each other cross?"
"Must every joy be dung & dross?"
"Must my dear Butts feel cold neglect"
"Because I give Hayley his due respect?"

"Must Flaxman look upon me as wild,"
"And all my friends be with doubts beguil'd?"
"Must my Wife live in my Sister's bane,"
"Or my Sister survive on my Love's pain?"
"The curses of Los the terrible shade"
"And his dismal terrors make me afraid."

So I spoke & struck in my wrath
The old man weltering upon my path.
Then Los appear'd in all his power:
In the Sun he appear'd, descending before
My face in fierce flames; in my double sight
'Twas outward a Sun: inward Los in his might.

"My hands are labour'd day & night,"
"And Ease comes never in my sight."
"My Wife has no indulgence given"
"Except what comes to her from heaven."
"We eat little, we drink less;"
"This Earth breeds not our happiness."
"Another Sun feeds our life's streams,"
"We are not warmed with thy beams;"
"Thou measurest not the Time to me,"
"Nor yet the Space that I do see;"

"My Mind is not with thy light array'd."
"Thy terrors shall not make me afraid."

When I had my Defiance given,
The Sun stood trembling in heaven;
The Moon that glow'd remote below,
Became leprous & white as snow;
And every soul of men on the Earth
Felt affliction & sorrow & sickness & dearth.
Los flam'd in my path, & the Sun was hot
With the bows of my Mind & the Arrows of Thought—
My bowstring fierce with Ardour breathes,
My arrows glow in their golden sheaves;
My brothers & father march before;
The heavens drop with human gore.

Now I a fourfold vision see,
And a fourfold vision is given to me;
'Tis fourfold in my supreme delight
And threefold in soft Beulah's night
And twofold Always. May God us keep
From Single vision & Newton's sleep!

From *Vala or the four Zoas*

LAMENTATION OF THE EARTH

"Why does the Raven cry aloud and no eye pities her?
"Why fall the Sparrow & the Robin in the foodless winter?
"Faint, shivering, they sit on leafless bush or frozen stone

"Wearied with seeking food across the snowy waste, the little
"Heart cold, and the little tongue consum'd that once in thought-
     less joy
"Gave songs of gratitude to waving cornfields round their nest.

"Why howl the Lion & the Wolf? why do they roam abroad?
"Deluded by summer's heat, they sport in enormous love
"And cast their young out to the hungry wilds & sandy desarts.

"Why is the Sheep given to the knife? the Lamb plays in the Sun:
"He starts! he hears the foot of Man! he says: Take thou my wool,
"But spare my life: *but* he knows not that winter cometh fast.

"The Spider sits on his labour'd Web, eager watching for the Fly.
"Presently comes a famish'd Bird & takes away the Spider.
"His Web is left all desolate that his little anxious heart
"So careful wove & spread it out with sighs and weariness."

This was the Lamentation of Enion round the golden Feast.

THUS WERE THE STARS OF HEAVEN CREATED

Thus were the stars of heaven created like a golden chain
To bind the Body of Man to heaven from falling into the Abyss.
Each took his station & his course began with sorrow & care.

In sevens & tens & fifties, hundreds, thousands, number'd all
According to their various powers, subordinate to Urizen
And to his sons in their degrees & to his beauteous daughters,
Travelling in silent majesty along their order'd ways
In right lined paths outmeasur'd by proportions of number, weight
And measure, mathematic motion wondrous along the deep,
In fiery pyramid, or Cube, or unornamented pillar square
Of fire, far shining, travelling along even to its destin'd end;
Then falling down a terrible space, recovering in winter dire
Its wasted strength, it back returns upon a nether course,
Till fir'd with ardour recruited in its humble season,
It rises up on high all summer, till its wearied course
Turns into autumn. Such the period of many worlds.
Others triangular, right angled course maintain. Others obtuse,
Acute, Scalene, in simple paths; but others move
In intricate ways, biquadrate, Trapeziums, Rhombs, Rhomboids,
Paralellograms triple & quadruple, polygonic
In their amazing hard subdu'd course in the vast deep.

THE SONG OF ENITHARMON

"I seize the sphery harp. I strike the strings

At the first sound the Golden sun arises from the deep
"And shakes his awful hair,
"The Eccho wakes the moon to unbind her silver locks,
"The golden sun bears on my song
"And nine bright spheres of harmony rise round the fiery king.

"The joy of woman is the death of her most best beloved
"Who dies for Love of her
"In torments of fierce jealousy & pangs of adoration.
"The Lovers' night bears on my song
"And the nine spheres rejoice beneath my powerful controll.

"They sing unceasing to the notes of my immortal hand.
"The solemn, silent moon
"Reverberates the living harmony upon my limbs,
"The birds & beasts rejoice & play,
"And every one seeks for his mate to prove his inmost joy.

"Furious & terrible they sport & rend the nether deeps;
"The deep lifts up his rugged head,
"And lost in infinite humming wings vanishes with a cry.
"The fading cry is ever dying,
"The living voice is ever living in its inmost joy.

"Arise, you little glancing wings & sing your infant joy!
"Arise & drink your bliss!
"For every thing that lives is holy; for the source of life
"Descends to be a weeping babe;
"For the Earthworm renews the moisture of the sandy plain.

"Now my left hand I stretch to earth beneath,
"And strike the terrible string.
"I wake sweet joy in dens of sorrow & I plant a smile
"In forests of affliction,
"And wake the bubbling springs of life in regions of dark death.

"O, I am weary! lay thine hand upon me or I faint,
"I faint beneath these beams of thine,
"For thou hast touch'd my five senses & they answer'd thee.
"Now I am nothing, & I sink
"And on the bed of silence sleep till thou awakest me."

THE PRICE OF EXPERIENCE

"I am made to sow the thistle for wheat, the nettle for a nourishing
        dainty.
"I have planted a false oath in the earth; it has brought forth a poi-
        son tree.
"I have chosen the serpent for a councellor, & the dog
"For a schoolmaster to my children.
"I have blotted out from light & living the dove & nightingale,
"And I have caused the earth worm to beg from door to door.

"I have taught the thief a secret path into the house of the just.
"I have taught pale artifice to spread his nets upon the morning.
"My heavens are brass, my earth is iron, my moon a clod of clay
"My sun a pestilence burning at noon & a vapour of death in night.

"What is the price of Experience? do men buy it for a song?
"Or wisdom for a dance in the street? No, it is bought with the
        price
"Of all that a man hath, his house, his wife, his children.
"Wisdom is sold in the desolate market where none come to buy,
"And in the wither'd field where the farmer plows for bread in vain.

"It is an easy thing to triumph in the summer's sun
"And in the vintage & to sing on the waggon loaded with corn.
"It is an easy thing to talk of patience to the afflicted,
"To speak the laws of prudence to the houseless wanderer,
"To listen to the hungry raven's cry in wintry season
"When the red blood is fill'd with wine & with the marrow of
    lambs.

"It is an easy thing to laugh at wrathful elements,
"To hear the dog howl at the wintry door, the ox in the slaughter
    house moan;
"To see a god on every wind & a blessing on every blast;
"To hear sounds of love in the thunder storm that destroys our
    enemies' house;
"To rejoice in the blight that covers his field, & the sickness that
    cuts off his children,
"While our olive & vine sing & laugh round our door, & our
    children bring fruits & flowers.

"Then the groan & the dolor are quite forgotten, & the slave grin-
    ding at the mill,
"And the captive in chains, & the poor in the prison, & the soldier
    in the field
"When the shatter'd bone hath laid him groaning among the
    happier dead.

"It is an easy thing to rejoice in the tents of prosperity:
"Thus could I sing & thus rejoice: but it is not so with me."

THE TERRORS OF THE ABYSS

For Urizen beheld the terrors of the Abyss wandering among
The ruin'd spirits, once his children & the children of Luvah.
Scar'd at the sound of their own sigh that seems to shake the immense
They wander Moping, in their heart a sun, a dreary moon,
A Universe of fiery constellations in their brain,
An earth of wintry woe beneath their feet, & round their loins

Waters or winds or clouds or brooding lightnings & pestilential
    plagues.
Beyond the bounds of their own self their senses cannot penetrate:
As the tree knows not what is outside of its leaves & bark
And yet it drinks the summer joy & fears the winter sorrow,
So, in the regions of the grave, none knows his dark compeer
Tho' he partakes of his dire woes & mutual returns the pang,
The throb, the dolor, the convulsion, in soul-sickening woes.

The horrid shapes & sights of torment in burning dungeons & in
Fetters of red hot iron; some with crowns of serpents & some
With monsters girding round their bosoms; some lying on beds of
    sulphur,
On racks & wheels ; he beheld women marching o'er burning wastes
Of Sand in bands of hundreds & of fifties & of thousands, strucken
    with
Lightnings which blazed after them upon their shoulders in their
    march
In successive volleys with loud thunders: swift flew the King of Light
Over the burning desarts; Then, the desarts pass'd, involv'd in
    clouds
Of smoke with myriads moping in the stifling vapours, Swift
Flew the King, tho' flag'd his powers, labouring till over rocks
And Mountains faint weary he wander'd where multitudes were shut
Up in the solid mountains & in rocks which heav'd with their
    torments.
Then came he among fiery cities & castles built of burning steel.
Then he beheld the forms of tygers & of Lions, dishumaniz'd men.
Many in serpents & in worms, stretched out enormous length
Over the sullen mould & slimy tracks, obstruct his way
Drawn out from deep to deep, woven by ribb'd
And scaled monsters or arm'd in iron shell, or shell of brass
Or gold; a glittering torment shining & hissing in eternal pain;
Some, columns of fire or of water, sometimes stretch'd out in heighth,
Sometimes in length, sometimes englobing, wandering in vain
    seeking for ease.
His voice to them was but an inarticulate thunder, for their Ears
Were heavy & dull, & their eyes & nostrils closed up.

92

Oft he stood by a howling victim Questioning in words
Soothing or Furious; no one answer'd; every one wrap'd up
In his own sorrow howl'd regardless of his words, nor voice
Of sweet response could he obtain, tho' oft assay'd with tears.
He knew they were his Children ruin'd in his ruin'd world.

Oft would he stand & question a fierce scorpion glowing with gold;
In vain; the terror heard not. Then a lion he would sieze
By the fierce mane, staying his howling course; in vain the voice
Of Urizen, in vain the Eloquent tongue. A Rock, a Cloud, a
    Mountain,
Were now not Vocal as in Climes of happy Eternity
Where the lamb replies to the infant voice, & the lion to the man of
    years
Giving them sweet instructions; where the Cloud, the River & the
    Field
Talk with the husbandman & shepherd. But these attack'd him sore,
Siezing upon his feet, & rending the sinews, that in Caves
He hid to recure his obstructed powers with rest & oblivion.

Here he had time enough to repent of his rashly threaten'd curse.
He saw them cur'sd beyond his Curse: his soul melted with fear.
He could not take their fetters off, for they grew from the soul,
Nor could he quench the fires, for they flam'd out from the heart. . .

URIZEN READ IN HIS BOOK OF BRASS

"Compell the poor to live upon a Crust of bread, by soft mild arts.
"Smile when they frown, frown when they smile; & when a man
    looks pale
"With labour & abstinence, say he looks healthy & happy;
"And when his children sicken, let them die; there are enough
"Born, even too many, & our Earth will be overrun
"Without these arts. If you would make the poor live with temper,
"With pomp give every crust of bread you give; with gracious
    cunning
"Magnify small gifts; reduce the man to want a gift, & then give
    with pomp.

93

"Say he smiles if you hear him sigh. If pale, say he is ruddy.
"Preach temperance : say he is overgorg'd & drowns his wit
"In strong drink, tho' you know that bread & water are all
"He can afford. Flatter his wife, pity his children, till we can
"Reduce all to our will, as spaniels are taught with art.

ENION REPLIES FROM THE CAVERNS OF THE GRAVE

The furrow'd field replies to the grave. I hear her reply to me :
"Behold the time approaches fast that thou shalt be as a thing
"Forgotten ; when one speaks of thee he will not be believ'd.
"When the man gently fades away in his immortality,
"When the mortal disappears in improved knowledge, cast away
"The former things, so shall the Mortal gently fade away
"And so become invisible to those who still remain
"Listen. I will tell thee what is done in the caverns of the grave.
"The Lamb of God has rent the Veil of Mystery, soon to return
"In Clouds & Fires around the rock & the Mysterious tree.
"And as the seed waits Eagerly watching for its flower & fruit,
"Anxious its little soul looks out into the clear expanse
"To see if hungry winds are abroad with their invisible army,
"So Man looks out in tree & herb & fish & bird & beast
"Collecting up the scatter'd portions of his immortal body
"Into the Elemental forms of every thing that grows.
"He tries the sullen north wind, riding on its angry furrows,
"The sultry south when the sun rises, & the angry east
"When the sun sets ; when the clods harden & the cattle stand
"Drooping & the birds hide in their silent nests, he stores his
        thoughts
"As in a store house in his memory ; he regulates the forms
"Of all beneath & all above, & in the gentle West
"Reposes where the Sun's heat dwells ; he rises to the Sun
"And to the Planets of the Night, & to the stars that gild
"The Zodiac, & the stars that sullen stand to north & south.
"He touches the remotest pole, & in the center weeps
"That Man should Labour & sorrow, & learn & forget, & return

"To the dark valley whence he came, to begin his labour anew.
"In pain he sighs, in pain he labours in his universe,
"Screaming in birds over the deep, & howling in the wolf
"Over the slain, & moaning in the cattle, & in the winds,
"And weeping over Orc & Urizen in clouds & flaming fires,
"And in the cries of birth & in the groans of death his voice
"Is heard throughout the Universe: wherever a grass grows
"Or a leaf buds, The Eternal Man is seen, is heard, is felt,
"And all his sorrows, till he reassumes his ancient bliss."

THE LAST JUDGMENT

And Los & Enitharmon builded Jerusalem, weeping
Over the Sepulcher & over the Crucified body
Which, to their Phantom Eyes, appear'd still in the Sepulcher;
But Jesus stood beside them in the spirit, separating
Their spirit from their body. Terrified at Non Existence,
For such they deem'd the death of the body, Los his vegetable hands
Outstretch'd; his right hand, branching out in fibrous strength,
Siez'd the Sun; His left hand, like dark roots, cover'd the Moon,
And tore them down, cracking the heavens across from immense to
    immense.
Then fell the fires of Eternity with loud & shrill
Sound of Loud Trumpet thundering along from heaven to heaven
A mighty sound articulate: "Awake, ye dead, & come
"To Judgment from the four winds! Awake & Come away!"
Folding like scrolls of the Enormous volume of Heaven & Earth,
With thunderous noise & dreadful shakings, rocking to & fro,
The heavens are shaken & the Earth removed from its place,
The foundations of the Eternal hills discover'd:
The thrones of Kings are shaken, they have lost their robes &
    crowns,
The poor smite their oppressors, they awake up to the harvest,
The naked warriors rush together down to the sea shore
Trembling before the multitudes of slaves now set at liberty:
They are become like wintry flocks, like forests strip'd of leaves:
The oppressed pursue like the wind; there is no room for escape.

The Spectre of Enitharmon, let loose on the troubled deep,
Wail'd shrill in the confusion, & the Spectre of Urthona
Reciev'd her in the darkening south; their bodies lost, they stood
Trembling & weak, a faint embrace, a fierce desire, as when
Two shadows mingle on a wall; they wail & shadowy tears
Fell down, & shadowy forms of joy mix'd with despair & grief—
Their bodies buried in the ruins of the Universe—
Mingled with the confusion. Who shall call them from the Grave?

Rahab & Tirzah wail aloud in the wild flames; they give up
    themselves to Consummation.

The books of Urizen unroll with dreadful noise; the folding
    Serpent
Of Orc began to Consume in fierce raving fire; his fierce flames
Issu'd on all sides, gathering strength in animating volumes,
Roaming abroad on all the winds, raging intense, reddening
Into resistless pillars of fire rolling round & round, gathering
Strengh from the Earths consumed & heavens & all hidden abysses,
Where'er the Eagle has Explor'd, or Lion or Tyger trod,
Or where the Comets of the night or stars of asterial day
Have shot their arrows or long beamed spears in wrath & fury.

And all the while the trumpet sounds, from the clotted gore &
    from the hollow den
Start forth the trembling millions into flames of mental fire,
Bathing their limbs in the bright visions of Eternity.
Then, like the doves from pillars of Smoke, the trembling families
Of women & children throughout every nation under heaven
Cling round the men in bands of twenties & of fifties, pale
As snow that falls around a leafless tree upon the green.
Their oppressors are fall'n, they have stricken them, they awake to
    life.
Yet pale the just man stands erect & looking up to heav'n.

THE GOLDEN FEAST

ENION *spoke saying:*

I

"O Dreams of Death ! the human form dissolving, companied
"By beasts & worms & creeping things & darkness & despair.
"The clouds fall off from my wet brow, the dust from my cold
    limbs
"Into the sea of Tharmas. Soon renew'd, a Golden Moth,
"I shall cast off my death clothes & Embrace Tharmas again.
"For Lo, the winter melted away upon the distant hills,
"And all the black mould sings." She speaks to her infant race;
    her milk
Descends down on the sand; the thirsty sand drinks & rejoices
Wondering to behold the Emmet, the Grasshopper, the jointed
    worm.
The roots shoot thick thro' the solid rocks, bursting their way
They cry out in joys of existence; the broad stems
Rear on the mountains stem after stem; the scaly newt creeps
From the stone, & the armed fly springs from the rocky crevice,
The spider, The bat burst from the harden'd slime, crying
To one another :"What are we & whence is our joy & delight?
"Lo, the little moss begins to spring, & the tender weed
"Creeps round our secret nest." Flocks brighten the Mountains,
Herds throng up the Valley, wild beasts fill the forests.

II

And One of the Eternals spoke. All was silent at the feast.

"Man is a Worm; wearied with joy, he seeks the caves of sleep
"Among the Flowers of Beulah, in his selfish cold repose
"Forsaking Brotherhood & Universal love, in selfish clay
"Folding the pure wings of his mind, seeking the places dark
"Abstracted from the roots of (Nature *del.*) Science; then inclos'd
    around
"In walls of Gold we cast him like a seed into the Earth
"Till times & spaces have pass'd over him; duly every morn
"We visit him, covering with a Veil the immortal seed;

"With windows from the inclement sky we cover him, & with walls
"And hearths protect the selfish terror, till divided all
"In families we see our shadows born, & thence we know ⎤ Ephesi -
"That Man subsists by Brotherhood & Universal Love. ⎟ ans iii c.
"We fall on one another's necks, more closely we embrace. ⎦ 10 v
"Not for ourselves, but for the Eternal family we live.
"Man liveth not by Self alone, but in his brother's face
"Each shall behold the Eternal Father & love & joy abound."

So spoke the Eternal at the Feast; they embrac'd the New born Man,
Calling him Brother, image of the Eternal Father; they sat down
At the immortal tables, sounding loud their instruments of joy,
Calling the Morning into Beulah; the Eternal Man rejoic'd.

When Morning dawn'd, The Eternals rose to labour at the Vintage.
Beneath they saw their sons & daughters, wond'ring inconcievable
At the dark myriads in shadows in the worlds beneath.

The morning dawn'd. Urizen rose, & in his hand the Flail
Sounds on the Floor, heard terrible by all beneath the heavens.
Dismal loud redounding, the nether floor shakes with the sound,
And all Nations were threshed out, & the stars thresh'd from their
husks.
Then Tharmas took the Winnowing fan; the winnowing wind
furious
Above, veer'd round by violent whirlwind, driven west & south,
Tossed the Nations like chaff into the seas of Tharmas.

III

THARMAS *cries*:

"Let the slave, grinding at the mill, run out into the field;
"Let him look up into the heavens & laugh in the bright air.
"Let the inchained soul, shut up in darkness & in sighing,
"Whose face has never seen a smile in thirty weary years,
"Rise & look out: his chains are loose, his dungeon doors are open;
"And let his wife & children return from the opressor's scourge.

"They look behind at every step & believe it is a dream.
"Are these the slaves that groan'd along the streets of Mystery?
"Where are your bonds & task masters? are these the prisoners?
"Where are your chains? where are your tears? why do you look
    around?
"If you are thirsty, there is the river: go, bathe your parched limbs,
"The good of all the Land is before you, for Mystery is no more."

Then All the Slaves from every Earth in the wide Universe
Sing a New Song, drowning confusion in its happy notes,
While the flail of Urizen sounded loud, & the winnowing wind of
    Tharmas
So loud, so clear in the wide heavens; & the song that they sung was
    this,
Composed by an African Black from the little Earth of Sotha:

"Aha! Aha! how came I here so soon in my sweet native land?
"How came I here? Methinks I am as I was in my youth
"When in my father's house I sat & heard his chearing voice.
"Methinks I see his flocks & herds & feel my limbs renew'd,
"And Lo, my Brethren in their tents, & their little ones around
    them!"

From *Milton*

And did those feet in ancient time
Walk upon England's mountains green?
And was the holy Lamb of God
On England's pleasant pastures seen?

And did the Countenance Divine
Shine forth upon our clouded hills?
And was Jerusalem builded here
Among these dark Satanic Mills?

Bring me my Bow of burning gold:
Bring me my Arrows of desire:
Bring me my Spear: O clouds unfold!
Bring me my Chariot of fire.

I will not cease from Mental Fight,
Nor shall my Sword sleep in my hand
Till we have built Jerusalem
In England's green & pleasant Land.

THE BINDING OF URIZEN

Urizen lay in darkness & solitude, in chains of the mind lock'd up
Los siez'd his Hammer & Tongs; he labour'd at his resolute Anvil
Among indefinite Druid rocks & snows of doubt & reasoning.

Refusing all Definite Form, the Abstract Horror roof'd, stony hard;
And a first Age passed over, & a State of dismal woe.

Down sunk with fright a red round Globe, hot burning, deep,
Deep down into the Abyss, panting, conglobing, trembling;
And a second Age passed over, & a State of dismal woe.

Rolling round into two little Orbs, & closed in two little Caves,
The Eyes beheld the Abyss, lest bones of solidness freeze over all;
And a third Age passed over, & a State of dismal woe.

From beneath his Orbs of Vision, Two Ears in close volutions
Shot spiring out in the deep darkness & petrified as they grew;
And a fourth Age passed over, & a State of dismal woe.

Hanging upon the wind, two nostrils bent down into the Deep;
And a fifth Age passed over, & a State of dismal woe.

In ghastly torment sick, a Tongue of hunger & thirst flamed out;
And a sixth Age passed over, & a State of dismal woe.

Enraged & stifled without & within, in terror & woe he threw his
Right Arm to the north, his left Arm to the south, & his Feet
Stamp'd the nether Abyss in trembling & howling & dismay;
And a seventh Age passed over, & a State of dismal woe.

LOS

I

While Los heard indistinct in fear, what time I bound my sandals
On to walk forward thro' Eternity, Los descended to me:
And Los behind me stood, a terrible flaming Sun, just close
Behind my back. I turned round in terror, and behold!
Los stood in that fierce glowing fire, & he also stoop'd down
And bound my sandals on in Udan-Adan; trembling I stood
Exceedingly with fear & terror, standing in the Vale
Of Lambeth; but he kissed me and wish'd me health,
And I became One Man with him arising in my strength.
'Twas too late now to recede. Los had enter'd into my soul:
His terrors now posses'd me whole! I arose in fury & strength.

"I am that Shadowy Prophet who Six Thousand Years ago
"Fell from my station in the Eternal bosom. Six Thousand Years
"Are finish'd. I return! both Time & Space obey my will.
"I in Six Thousand Years walk up and down; for not one
       Moment
"Of Time is lost, nor one Event of Space unpermanent,
"But all remain: every fabric of Six Thousand Years
"Remains permanent, tho' on the Earth where Satan
"Fell and was cut off, all things vanish & are seen no more,
"They vanish not from me & mine, we guard them first & last.
"The generations of men run on in the tide of Time,
"But leave their destin'd lineaments permanent for ever & ever."

So spoke Los as we went along to his supreme abode.

Los is by mortals nam'd Time, Enitharmon is nam'd Space:
But they depict him bald & aged who is eternal youth
All powerful and his locks flourish like the brows of morning:
He is the Spirit of Prophecy, the ever apparent Elias.
Time is the mercy of Eternity; without Time's swiftness,
Which is the swiftest of all things, all were eternal torment.

All the Gods of the Kingdoms of Earth labour in Los's Halls:
Every one is a fallen Son of the Spirit of Prophecy.
He is the Fourth Zoa that stood around the Throne Divine.

AH WEAK & WIDE ASTRAY

"Ah weak & wide astray! Ah shut in narrow doleful form,
"Creeping in reptile flesh upon the bosom of the ground!
"The Eye of Man a little narrow orb, clos'd up & dark,
"Scarcely beholding the great light, conversing with the Void;
"The Ear a little shell, in small volutions shutting out
"All melodies & comprehending only Discord and Harmony;
"The Tongue a little moisture fills, a little food it cloys,
"A little sound it utters & its cries are faintly heard,
"Then brings forth Moral Virtue the cruel Virgin Babylon.

"Can such an Eye judge of the stars? & looking thro' its tubes
"Measure the sunny rays that point their spears on Udanadan?
"Can such an Ear, fill'd with the vapours of the yawning pit,
"Judge of the pure melodious harp struck by a hand divine?
"Can such closed Nostrils feel a joy? or tell of autumn fruits
"When grapes & figs burst their covering to the joyful air?
"Can such a Tongue boast of the living waters? or take in
"Ought but the Vegetable Ratio & loathe the faint delight?
"Can such gross Lips percieve? alas, folded within themselves
"They touch not ought, but pallid turn & tremble at every wind."

"Seeing the Churches at their Period in terror & despair,
"Rahab created Voltaire, Tirzah created Rousseau,
"Asserting the Self-righteousness against the Universal Saviour,
"Mocking the Confessors & Martyrs, claiming Self-righteousness,
"With cruel Virtue making War upon the Lamb's Redeemed
"To perpetuate War & Glory, to perpetuate the Laws of Sin.
"They perverted Swedenborg's Visions in Beulah & in Ulro
"To destroy Jerusalem as a Harlot & her Sons as Reprobates,
"To raise up Mystery the Virgin Harlot, Mother of War,
"Babylon the Great, the Abomination of Desolation.
"O Swedenborg! strongest of men, the Samson shorn by the
      Churches,
"Shewing the Transgressors in Hell, the proud Warriors in
      Heaven,
"Heaven as a Punisher, & Hell as One under Punishment,
"With Laws from Plato & his Greeks to renew the Trojan Gods
"In Albion, & to deny the value of the Saviour's blood.
"But then I rais'd up Whitefield, Palamabron rais'd up Westley.
"And these are the cries of the Churches before the two Witnesses.
"Faith in God the dear Saviour who took on the likeness of men,
"Becoming obedient to death, even the death of the Cross.
"The Witnesses lie dead in the Street of the Great City:
"No Faith is in all the Earth: the Book of God is trodden under
      Foot.
"He sent his two Servants, Whitefield & Westley: were they
      Prophets,
"Or were they Idiots or Madmen? shew us Miracles!
"Can you have greater Miracles than these? Men who devote
"Their life's whole comfort to intire scorn & injury & death?
"Awake, thou sleeper on the Rock of Eternity! Albion awake!"

THE WINE-PRESS

This Wine-press is call'd War on Earth: it is the Printing-Press
Of Los, and here he lays his words in order above the mortal brain,
As cogs are form'd in a wheel to turn the cogs of the adverse wheel.

Timbrels & violins sport round the Wine-presses; the little Seed,
The sportive Root, the Earth-worm, the gold Beetle, the wise Emmet,
Dance round the Wine-presses of Luvah: the Centipede is there,
The ground Spider with many eyes, the Mole clothed in velvet,
The ambitious Spider in his sullen web, the lucky golden Spinner,
The Earwig arm'd, the tender Maggot, emblem of immortality,
The Flea, Louse, Bug, the Tape-Worm, all the Armies of Disease,
Visible or invisible to the slothful vegetating Man.
The slow Slug, the Grasshopper that sings & laughs & drinks:
Winter comes, he folds his slender bones without a murmur.
The cruel Scorpion is there, the Gnat, Wasp, Hornet & the Honey
    Bee,
The Toad & venomous Newt, the Serpent cloth'd in gems & gold.
They throw off their gorgeous raiment: they rejoice with loud
    jubilee
Around the Wine-presses of Luvah, naked & drunk with wine.

There is the Nettle that sings with soft down, and there
The indignant Thistle whose bitterness is bred in his milk,
Who feeds on contempt of his neighbour: there all the idle Weeds
That creep around the obscure places shew their various limbs
Naked in all their beauty dancing round the Wine-presses.

But in the Wine-presses the Human grapes sing not nor dance:
They howl & writhe in shoals of torment, in fierce flames
    consuming....

THE SONS OF LOS
(1)

Thou seest the Constellations in the deep & wondrous Night:
They rise in order and continue their immortal courses
Upon the mountain & in vales with harp & heavenly song,
With flute & clarion, with cups & measures fill'd with foaming
    wine.
Glitt'ring the streams reflect the Vision of beatitude,
And the calm Ocean joys beneath & smooths his awful waves:

These are the Sons of Los, & these the Labourers of the Vintage.
Thou seest the gorgeous clothed Flies that dance & sport in summer
Upon the sunny brooks & meadows: every one the dance
Knows in its intricate mazes of delight artful to weave:
Each one to sound his instruments of music in the dance,
To touch each other & recede, to cross & change & return:
These are the Children of Los; thou seest the Trees on mountains,
The wind blows heavy, loud they thunder thro' the darksom sky,
Uttering prophecies & speaking instructive words to the sons
Of men: These are the Sons of Los: These the Visions of Eternity,
But we see only as it were the hem of their garments
When with our vegetable eyes we view these wondrous Visions.

(2)

Some Sons of Los surrond the Passions with porches of iron &
    silver,
Creating form & beauty around the dark regions of sorrow,
Giving to airy nothing a name and a habitation
Delightful, with bounds to the Infinite putting off the Indefinite
Into most holy forms of Thought; such is the power of inspiration.
They labour incessant with many tears & afflictions,
Creating the beautiful House for the piteous sufferer.

Others Cabinets richly fabricate of gold & ivory
For Doubts & fears unform'd & wretched & melancholy.
The little weeping Spectre stands on the threshold of Death
Eternal, and sometimes two Spectres like lamps quivering,
And often malignant they combat; heart-breaking sorrowful &
    piteous,
Antamon takes them into his beautiful flexible hands:
As the Sower takes the seed or as the Artist his clay
Or fine wax, to mould artful a model for golden ornaments.
The soft hands of Antamon draw the indelible line,

Form immortal with golden pen, such as the Spectre admiring
Puts on the sweet form; then smiles Antamon bright thro' his
    windows.
The Daughters of beauty look up from their Loom & prepare
The integument soft for its clothing with joy & delight.

But Theotormon & Sotha stand in the Gate of Luban anxious.
Their numbers are seven million & seven thousand & seven hundred.
They contend with the weak Spectres, they fabricate soothing forms.
The Spectre refuses, he seeks cruelty: they create the crested Cock.
Terrified the Spectre screams & rushes in fear into their Net
Of kindness & compassion, & is born a weeping terror.
Or they create the Lion & Tyger in compassionate thunderings:
Howling the Spectres flee: they take refuge in Human lineaments.

The Sons of Ozoth within the Optic Nerve stand fiery glowing,
And the number of his Sons is eight millions & eight.
They give delights to the man unknown; artificial riches
They give to scorn, & their possessors to trouble & sorrow & care,
Shutting the sun & moon & stars & trees & clouds & waters
And hills out from the Optic Nerve, & hardening it into a bone
Opake and like the black pebble on the enraged beach,
While the poor indigent is like the diamond which, tho' cloth'd
In rugged covering in the mine, is open all within
And in his hallow'd center holds the heavens of bright eternity.
Ozoth here builds walls of rocks against the surging sea,
And timbers crampt with iron cramps bar in the joys of life
From fell destruction in the Spectrous cunning or rage. He Creates
The speckled Newt, the Spider & Beetle, the Rat & Mouse,
The Badger & Fox: they worship before his feet in trembling fear.

    But others of the Sons of Los build Moments & Minutes & Hours
And Days & Months & Years & Ages & Periods, wondrous
    buildings;
And every Moment has a Couch of gold for soft repose,
(A Moment equals a pulsation of the artery),
And between every two Moments stands a Daughter of Beulah
To feed the Sleepers on their Couches with maternal care.

And every Minute has an azure Tent with silken Veils:
And every Hour has a bright golden Gate carved with skill:
And every Day & Night has Walls of brass & Gates of adamant,
Shining like precious Stones & ornamented with appropriate signs:
And every Month a silver paved Terrace builded high:
And every Year invulnerable Barriers with high Towers:
And every Age is Moated deep with Bridges of silver & gold:
And every Seven Ages is Incircled with a Flaming Fire.
Now Seven Ages is amounting to Two Hundred Years.
Each has its Guard, each Moment, Minute, Hour, Day, Month &
     Year.
All are the work of Fairy hands of the Four Elements:
The Guard are Angels of Providence on duty evermore.
Every Time less than a pulsation of the artery
Is equal in its period & value to Six Thousand Years,
For in this Period the Poet's Work is Done, and all the Great
Events of Time start forth & are conciev'd in such a Period,
Within a Moment, a Pulsation of the Artery.

The Sky is an immortal Tent built by the Sons of Los:
And every Space that a Man views around his dwelling-place
Standing on his own roof or in his garden on a mount
Of twenty-five cubits in height, such is his Universe:
And on its verge the sun rises & sets, the Clouds bow
To meet the flat Earth & the Sea in such an order'd Space:
The Starry heavens reach no further, but here bend and set
On all sides, & the two Poles turn on their valves of gold;
And if he move his dwelling-place, his heavens also move
Where'er he goes, & all his neighbourhood bewail his loss.
Such are the Spaces called Earth & such its dimension.
As to that false appearance which appears to the reasoner
As of a Globe rolling thro' Voidness, it is a delusion of Ulro.
The Microscope knows not of this nor the Telescope: they alter
The ratio of the Spectator's Organs, but leave Objects untouch'd.
For every Space larger than a red Globule of Man's blood
Is visionary, and is created by the Hammer of Los:
And every Space smaller than a Globule of Man's blood opens

Into Eternity of which this vegetable Earth is but a shadow.
The red Globule is the unwearied Sun by Los created
To measure Time and Space to mortal Men every morning.

THE CHOIR OF DAY

Thou hearest the Nightingale begin the Song of Spring.
The Lark sitting upon his earthy bed, just as the morn
Appears, listens silent; then springing from the waving Cornfield,
    loud
He leads the Choir of Day: trill, trill, trill, trill,
Mounting upon the wings of light into the Great Expanse,
Reecchoing against the lovely blue & shining heavenly Shell,
His little throat labours with inspiration; every feather
On throat & breast & wings vibrates with the effluence Divine.
All Nature listens silent to him, & the awful Sun
Stands still upon the Mountain looking on this little Bird
With eyes of soft humility & wonder, love & awe.
Then loud from their green covert all the Birds begin their Song:
The Thrush, the Linnet & the Goldfinch, Robin, & the Wren
Awake the Sun from his sweet reverie upon the Mountain.
The Nightingale again assays his song, & thro' the day
And thro' the night warbles luxuriant, every Bird of Song
Attending his loud harmony with admiration & love.
This is a Vision of the lamentation of Beulah over Ololon.

Thou percievest the Flowers put forth their precious Odours,
And none can tell how from so small a center comes such sweets,
Forgetting that within that Center Eternity expands
Its ever during doors that Og & Anak fiercely guard.
First, e'er the morning breaks, joy opens in the flowery bosoms,
Joy even to tears, which the Sun rising dries; first the Wild Thyme
And Meadow-sweet, downy & soft waving among the reeds,
Light springing on the air, lead the sweet Dance: they wake
The Honeysuckle sleeping on the Oak; the flaunting beauty
Revels along upon the wind; the White-thorn, lovely May,

Opens her many lovely eyes listening; the Rose still sleeps,
None dare to wake her; soon she bursts her crimson curtain'd bed
And comes forth in the majesty of beauty; every Flower,
The Pink, the Jessamine, the Wall-flower, the Carnation,
The Jonquil, the mild Lilly, opes her heavens; every Tree
And Flower & Herb soon fill the air with an innumerable Dance,
Yet all in order sweet & lovely. Men are sick with Love.
Such is a Vision of the lamentation of Beulah over Ololon.

THE SEVEN ANGELS OF THE PRESENCE INSTRUCT MILTON

And thus the Seven Angels instructed him, & thus they converse:

"We are not Individuals but States, Combinations of Individuals.
"We were Angels of the Divine Presence, & were Druids in
      Annandale,
"Compell'd to combine into Form by Satan, the Spectre of Albion,
"Who made himself a God & destroyed the Human Form Divine.
"But the Divine Humanity & Mercy gave us a Human   כדכ׳ס
      Form
"as multitudes
"Vox Populi
"Because we were combin'd in Freedom & holy
      Brotherhood,
"While those combin'd by Satan's Tyranny, first in the blood of
      War
"And Sacrifice & next in Chains of imprisonment, are Shapeless
      Rocks

"Retaining only Satan's Mathematic Holiness, Length, Bredth &
      Highth,
"Calling the Human Imagination, which is the Divine Vision &
      Fruition
"In which Man liveth eternally, madness & blasphemy against
"Its own Qualities, which are Servants of Humanity, not Gods or
      Lords.
"Distinguish therefore States from Individuals in those States.

"States Change, but Individual Identities never change nor cease.
"You cannot go to Eternal Death in that which can never Die.
"Satan & Adam are States Created into Twenty-seven Churches,
"And thou, O Milton, art a State about to be Created,

"Called Eternal Annihilation, that none but the Living shall
"Dare to enter, & they shall enter triumphant over Death
"And Hell & the Grave: States that are not, but ah ! Seem to be.

"Judge then of thy Own Self: thy Eternal Lineaments explore,
"What is Eternal & what Changeable,& what Annihilable.
"The Imagination is not a State: it is the Human Existence itself.
"Affection or Love becomes a State when divided from Imagination.
"The Memory is a State always, & the Reason is a State
"Created to be Annihilated & a new Ratio Created.
"Whatever can be Created can be Annihilated: Forms cannot:
"The Oak is cut down by the Ax, the Lamb falls by the Knife,
"But their Forms Eternal Exist For-ever. Amen. Hallelujah !"

Thus they converse with the Dead, watching round the Couch of
    Death;
For God himself enters Death's Door always with those that enter
And lays down in the Grave with them, in Visions of Eternity,
Till they awake & see Jesus & the Linen Clothes lying
That the Females had Woven for them, & the Gates of their
    Father's House.

THE GRANDEUR OF INSPIRATION

But turning toward Ololon in terrible majesty Milton
Replied: "Obey thou the Words of the Inspired Man.
"All that can be can be annihilated must be annihilated
"That the Children of Jerusalem may be saved from slavery.
"There is a Negation, & there is a Contrary:
"The Negation must be destroyed to redeem the Contraries.
"The Negation is the Spectre, the Reasoning Power in Man:
"This is a false Body, an Incrustation over my Immortal

"Spirit, a Selfhood which must be put off & annihilated alway.
"To cleanse the Face of my Spirit by Self-examination,
"To bathe in the Waters of Life, to wash off the Not Human,
"I come in Self-annihilation & the grandeur of Inspiration,
"To cast off Rational Demonstration by Faith in the Saviour,
"To cast off the rotten rags of Memory by Inspiration,
"To cast off Bacon, Locke & Newton from Albion's covering,
"To take off his filthy garments & clothe him with Imagination,
"To cast aside from Poetry all that is not Inspiration,
"That it no longer shall dare to mock with the aspersion of Madness
"Cast on the Inspired by the tame high finisher of paltry Blots
"Indefinite, or paltry Rhymes, or paltry Harmonies,
"Who creeps into State Government like a catterpiller to destroy ;
"To cast off the idiot Questioner who is always questioning
"But never capable of answering, who sits with a sly grin
"Silent plotting when to question, like a thief in a cave,
"Who publishes doubt & calls it knowledge, whose Science is
    Despair,
"Whose pretence to knowledge is envy, whose whole Science is
"To destroy the wisdom of ages to gratify ravenous Envy
"That rages round him like a Wolf day & night without rest :
"He smiles with condescension, he talks of Benevolence & Virtue,
"And those who act with Benevolence & Virtue they murder time
    on time.
"These are the destroyers of Jerusalem, these are the murderers
"Of Jesus, who deny the Faith & mock at Eternal Life,
"Who pretend to Poetry that they may destroy Imagination
"By imitation of Nature's Images drawn from Remembrance.
"These are the Sexual Garments, the Abomination of Desolation,
"Hiding the Human Lineaments as with an Ark & Curtains
"Which Jesus rent & now shall wholly purge away with Fire
"Till Generation is swallow'd up in Regeneration."

From *Jerusalem*

INVOCATION

Trembling I sit day and night, my friends are astonish'd at me,
Yet they forgive my wanderings. I rest not from my great task!
To open the Eternal Worlds, to open the immortal Eyes
Of Man inwards into the Worlds of Thought, into Eternity
Ever expanding in the Bosom of God, the Human Imagination.
O Saviour pour upon me thy Spirit of meekness & love!
Annihilate the Selfhood in me: be thou my life!
Guide thou my hand, which trembles exceedingly upon the rock
    of ages,
While I write of the building of Golgonooza, & of the terrors of
    Entuthon,
Of Hand & Hyle & Coban, of Kwantok, Peachey, Brereton,
    Slayd & Hutton,
Of the terrible sons & daughters of Albion, and their Generations.

O HOLY GENERATION

"Pity must join together those whom wrath has torn in sunder,
"And the Religion of Generation, which was meant for the
    destruction
"Of Jerusalem, become her covering till the time of the End
"O holy Generation, Image of regeneration!
"O point of mutual forgiveness between Enemies!
"Birthplace of the Lamb of God incomprehensible!
"The Dead despise & scorn thee & cast thee out as accursed,
"Seeing the Lamb of God in thy gardens & thy palaces
"Where they desire to place the Abomination of Desolation.

LONDON'S GOLDEN BUILDERS

What are those golden builders doing? where was the burying-
place
Of soft Enthinthus? near Tyburn's fatal Tree? is that
Mild Zion's hill's most ancient promontory, near mournful
Ever weeping Paddington? is that Calvary and Golgotha
Becoming a building of pity and compassion? Lo!
The stones are pity, and the bricks, well wrought affections
Enamel'd with love & kindness, & the tiles engraven gold,
Labour of merciful hands: the beams & rafters are forgiveness:
The mortar & cement of the work, tears of honesty: the nails
And the screws & iron braces are well wrought blandishments
And well contrived words, firm fixing, never forgotten,
Always comforting the remembrance: the floors, humility:
The cielings, devotion: the hearths, thanksgiving.
Prepare the furniture, O Lambeth, in thy pitying looms,
The curtains, woven tears & sighs wrought into lovely forms
For comfort; there the secret furniture of Jerusalem's chamber
Is wrought. Lambeth! the Bride, the Lamb's Wife, loveth thee.
Thou art one with her & knowest not of self in thy supreme joy.
Go on, builders in hope, tho' Jerusalem wanders far away
Without the gate of Los, among the dark Satanic wheels.

THE FOURFOLD MAN

And Los beheld his Sons and he beheld his Daughters,
Every one a translucent Wonder, a Universe within,
Increasing inwards into length and breadth and heighth,
Starry & glorious; and they every one in their bright loins
Have a beautiful golden gate, which opens into the vegetative world;
And every one a gate of rubies & all sorts of precious stones
In their translucent hearts, which opens into the vegetative world;
And every one a gate of iron dreadful and wonderful
In their translucent heads, which opens into the vegetative world;

And every one has the three regions, Childhood, Manhood & Age;
But the gate of the tongue, the western gate, in them is clos'd,
Having a wall builded against it, and thereby the gates
Eastward & Southward & Northward are incircled with flaming
    fires,
And the North is Breadth, the South is Heighth & Depth,
The East is Inwards, & the West is Outwards every way.

II

I see the Four-fold Man, The Humanity in deadly sleep
And its fallen Emanation, The Spectre & its cruel Shadow.
I see the Past, Present & Future existing all at once
Before me. O Divine Spirit, sustain me on thy wings,
That I may awake Albion from his long & cold repose;
For Bacon & Newton, sheath'd in dismal steel, their terrors hang
Like iron scourges over Albion: Reasonings like vast Serpents
Infold around my limbs, bruising my minute articulations.

I turn my eyes to the Schools & Universities of Europe
And there behold the Loom of Locke, whose Woof rages dire,
Wash'd by the Water-wheels of Newton: black the cloth
In heavy wreathes folds over every Nation: cruel Works
Of many Wheels I view, wheel without wheel, with cogs tyrannic
Moving by compulsion each other, not as those in Eden, which,
Wheel within Wheel, in freedom revolve in harmony & peace.

LOS'S HALLS
I

There is the Cave, the Rock, the Tree, the Lake of Udan Adan
The Forest and the Marsh and the Pits of bitumen deadly,
The Rocks of solid fire, the Ice valleys, the Plains
Of burning sand, the rivers, cataract & Lakes of Fire,
The Islands of the fiery Lakes, the Trees of Malice, Revenge
And black Anxiety, and the Cities of the Salamandrine men,
(But whatever is visible to the Generated Man
Is a Creation of mercy & love from the Satanic Void).

The land of darkness flamed, but no light & no repose:
The land of snows of trembling & of iron hail incessant:
The land of earthquakes, and the land of woven labyrinths:
The land of snares & traps & wheels & pit-falls & dire mills:
The Voids, the Solids, & the land of clouds & regions of waters
With their inhabitants, in the Twenty-seven Heavens beneath
    Beulah:
Self-righteousnesses conglomerating against the Divine Vision:
A Concave Earth wondrous, Chasmal, Abyssal, Incoherent,
Forming the Mundane Shell: above, beneath, an all sides surroun-
    ding
Golgonooza. Los walks round the walls night and day.

He views the City of Golgonooza & its smaller Cities,
The Looms & Mills & Prisons & Work-houses of Og & Anak,
The Amalekite, the Canaanite, the Moabite, the Egyptian,
And all that has existed in the space of six thousand years,
Permanent & not lost, not lost nor vanish'd, & every little act,
Word, work & wish that has existed, all remaining still
In those Churches ever consuming & ever building by the Spectres
Of all the inhabitants of Earth wailing to be Created,
Shadowy to those who dwell not in them, meer possibilities,
But to those who enter into them they seem the only substances;
For every thing exists & not one sigh nor smile nor tear,
One hair nor particle of dust, not one can pass away.

II

All things acted on Earth are seen in the bright Sculptures of
Los's Halls, & every Age renews its powers from these Works
With every pathetic story possible to happen from Hate or
Wayward Love; & every sorrow & distress is carved here,
Every Affinity of parents, Marriages & Friendships are here
In all their various combinations wrought with wonderous Art,
All that can happen to Man in his pilgrimage of seventy years.
Such is the Divine Written Law of Horeb & Sinai,
And such the Holy Gospel of Mount Olivet & Calvary.

THE FIELDS FROM ISLINGTON
TO MARYBONE

The fields from Islington to Marybone,
To Primrose Hill and Saint John's Wood,
 Were builded over with pillars of gold,
And there Jerusalem's pillars stood.

Her Little-ones ran on the fields,
The Lamb of God among them seen,
 And fair Jerusalem his Bride,
Among the little meadows green.

Pancrass & Kentish-town repose
Among her golden pillars high,
 Among her golden arches which
Shine upon the starry sky.

The Jew's-harp-house & the Green Man,
The Ponds where Boys to bathe delight,
 The fields of Cows by Willan's farm,
Shine in Jerusalem's pleasant sight.

She walks upon our meadows green,
The Lamb of God walks by her side,
 And every English Child is seen
Children of Jesus & his Bride.

Forgiving trespasses and sins
Lest Babylon with cruel Og
 With Moral & Self-righteous Law
Should Crucify in Satan's Synagogue!

What are those golden Builders doing
Near mournful ever-weeping Paddington,
 Standing above that mighty Ruin
Where Satan the first victory won,

Where Albion slept beneath the Fatal Tree,
And the Druids' golden Knife
 Rioted in human gore,
In Offerings of Human Life?

They groan'd aloud on London Stone,
They groan'd aloud on Tyburn's Brook,
  Albion gave his deadly groan,
And all the Atlantic Mountains shook.

Albion's Spectre from his Loins
Tore forth in all the pomp of War:
  Satan his name: in flames of fire
He stretch'd his Druid Pillars far,

Jerusalem fell from Lambeth's Vale
Down thro' Poplar & Old Bow,
  Thro' Malden & across the Sea,
In War & howling, death & woe.

The Rhine was red with human blood,
The Danube roll'd a purple tide,
  On the Euphrates Satan stood,
And over Asia stretch'd his pride.

He wither'd up sweet Zion's Hill
From every Nation of the Earth;
  He wither'd up Jerusalem's Gates,
And in a dark Land gave her birth.

He wither'd up the Human Form
By laws of sacrifice for sin,
  Till it became a Mortal Worm,
But O! translucent all within.

The Divine Vision still was seen,
Still was the Human Form Divine,
  Weeping in weak & mortal clay,
O Jesus, still the Form was thine.

And thine the Human Face, & thine
The Human Hands & Feet & Breath,
  Entering thro' the Gates of Birth
And passing thro' the Gates of Death.

And O thou Lamb of God, whom I
Slew in my dark self-righteous pride,
    Art thou return'd to Albion's Land?
And is Jerusalem thy Bride?

Come to my arms & never more
Depart, but dwell for ever here:
    Create my Spirit to thy Love:
Subdue my Spectre to thy Fear.

Spectre of Albion! warlike Fiend!
In clouds of blood & ruin roll'd,
    I here reclaim thee as my own,
My Self-hood! Satan! arm'd in gold.

Is this thy soft Family-Love,
Thy cruel Patriarchal pride,
    Planting thy Family alone,
Destroying all the World beside?

A man's worst enemies are those
Of his own house & family;
    And he who makes his law a curse,
By his own law shall surely die.

In my Exchanges every Land
Shall walk, & mine in every Land,
    Mutual shall build Jerusalem,
Both heart in heart & hand in hand.

SO SPOKE THE SPECTRE

Turning his back to the Divine Vision, his Spectrous
Chaos before his face appear'd, an Unformed Memory.

Then spoke the Spectrous Chaos to Albion, dark'ning cold,
From the back & loins where dwell the Spectrous Dead:

"I am your Rational Power, O Albion, & that Human Form
"You call Divine is but a Worm seventy inches long
"That creeps forth in a night & is dried in the morning sun,
"In fortuitous concourse of memorys accumulated & lost.
"It plows the Earth in its own conceit, it overwhelms the Hills
"Beneath its winding labyrinths, till a stone of the brook
"Stops it in midst of its pride among its hills & rivers.
"Battersea & Chelsea mourn, London & Canterbury tremble:
"Their place shall not be found as the wind passes over.
"The ancient Cities of the Earth remove as a traveller,
"And shall Albion's Cities remain when I pass over them
"With my deluge of forgotten remembrances over the tablet?"

So spoke the Spectre to Albion: he is the Great Selfhood,
Satan, Worship'd as God by the Mighty Ones of the Earth . . .

CONSIDER THIS

If Perceptive Organs vary, Objects of Perception seem to vary:
If the Perceptive Organs close, their Objects seem to close also.
"Consider this, O mortal Man, O worm of sixty winters," said
  Los,
"Consider Sexual Organization & hide thee in the dust."

WHAT SEEMS TO BE, IS

Then those in Great Eternity who contemplate on Death
Said thus: "What seems to Be, Is, To those to whom
"It seems to Be, & is productive of the most dreadful
"Consequences to those to whom it seems to Be, even of
"Torments, Despair, Eternal Death; but the Divine Mercy

"Steps beyond and Redeems Man in the Body of Jesus. Amen.
"And Length, Bredth, Highth again Obey the Divine Vision.
  Hallelujah."

Turning from Universal Love, petrific as he went,
His cold against the warmth of Eden rag'd with loud
Thunders of deadly war (the fever of the human soul)
Fires and clouds of rolling smoke! but mild, the Saviour follow'd
    him,
Displaying the Eternal Vision, the Divine Similitude,
In loves and tears of brothers, sisters, sons, fathers and friends,
Which if Man ceases to behold, he ceases to exist,

Saying, "Albion! Our wars are wars of life, & wounds of love
"With intellectual spears, & long winged arrows of thought.
"Mutual in one another's love and wrath all renewing
"We live as One Man; for contracting our infinite senses
"We behold multitude, or expanding, we behold as one,
"As One Man all the Universal Family, and that One Man

"We call Jesus the Christ; and he in us, and we in him
"Live in perfect harmony in Eden, the land of life,
"Giving, recieving, and forgiving each other's trespasses.
"He is the Good shepherd, he is the Lord and master,
"He is the Shepherd of Albion, he is all in all,
"In Eden, in the garden of God, and in heavenly Jerusalem.
"If we have offended, forgive us; take not vengeance against us."

Thus speaking, the Divine Family follow Albion.
I see them in the Vision of God upon my pleasant valleys.

I behold London, a Human awful wonder of God!
He says: "Return, Albion, return! I give myself for thee.
"My Streets are my Ideas of Imagination.
"Awake Albion, awake! and let us awake up together.
"My Houses are Thoughts: my Inhabitants, Affections,
"The children of my thoughts walking within my blood-vessels,
"Shut from my nervous form which sleeps upon the verge of
    Beulah
"In dreams of darkness, while my vegetating blood in veiny pipes

"Rolls dreadful thro' the Furnaces of Los and the Mills of Satan.
"For Albion's sake and for Jerusalem thy Emanation
"I give myself, and these my brethren give themselves for Albion."

So spoke London, immortal Guardian! I heard in Lambeth's
    shades.
In Felpham I heard and saw the Visions of Albion.
I write in South Molton Street what I both see and hear
In regions of Humanity, in London's opening streets.

I see thee, awful Parent Land in light, behold I see!
Verulam! Canterbury! venerable parent of men,
Generous immortal Guardian, golden clad! for Cities
Are Men, fathers of multitudes, and Rivers & Mountains
Are also Men; every thing is Human, mighty! sublime!
In every bosom a Universe expands as wings,
Let down at will around and call'd the Universal Tent.
York, crown'd with loving kindness, Edinburgh, cloth'd
With fortitude, as with a garment of immortal texture
Woven in looms of Eden, in spiritual deaths of mighty men
Who give themselves in Golgotha, Victims to Justice, where
There is in Albion a Gate of Precious stones and gold
Seen only by Emanations, by vegetations viewless:
Bending across the road of Oxford Street, it from Hyde Park
To Tyburn's deathful shades admits the wandering souls
Of multitudes who die from Earth: this Gate cannot be found

By Satan's Watch-fiends, tho' they search numbering every grain
Of sand on Earth every night, they never find this Gate.
It is the Gate of Los. Withoutside is the Mill, intricate, dreadful
And fill'd with cruel tortures; but no mortal man can find the Mill
Of Satan in his mortal pilgrimage of seventy years,
For Human beauty knows it not, nor can Mercy find it!...

ERIN SPOKE TO THE DAUGHTERS
OF BEULAH

"Remove from Albion, far remove these terrible surfaces:
"They are beginning to form Heavens & Hells in immense
"Circles, the Hells for food to the Heavens, food of torment,
"Food of despair: they drink the condemn'd Soul & rejoice
"In cruel holiness in their Heavens of Chastity & Uncircumcision
"Yet they are blameless, & Iniquity must be imputed only
"To the State they are enter'd into, that they may be deliver'd.
"Satan is the State of Death & not a Human existence;
"But Luvah is named Satan because he has enter'd that State:
"A World where Man is by Nature the enemy of Man,
"Because the Evil is Created into a State, that Men
"May be deliver'd time after time, evermore. Amen
"Learn therefore, O Sisters, to distinguish the Eternal Human
"That walks about among the stones of fire in bliss & woe
"Alternate, from those States or Worlds in which the Spirit travels.
"This is the only means to Forgiveness of Enemies.

I SAW A MONK OF CHARLEMAINE

I saw a Monk of Charlemaine
Arise before my sight:
I talk'd with the Grey Monk as we stood
In beams of infernal light.

Gibbon arose with a lash of steel,
And Voltaire with a wracking wheel;
The Schools, in clouds of learning roll'd,
Arose with War in iron & gold.

"Thou lazy Monk," they sound afar,
"In vain condemning glorious War;
"And in your Cell you shall ever dwell:
"Rise, War, & bind him in his Cell!"

The blood red ran from the Grey Monk's side,
His hands & feet were wounded wide,
    His body bent, his arms & knees
Like to the roots of ancient trees.

When Satan first the black bow bent
And the Moral Law from the Gospel rent,
    He forg'd the Law into a Sword
And spill'd the blood of mercy's Lord.

Titus! Constantine! Charlemaine!
O Voltaire! Rousseau! Gibbon! Vain
    Your Grecian Mocks & Roman Sword
Against this image of his Lord!

For a Tear is an Intellectual thing,
And a Sigh is the Sword of an Angel King,
    And the bitter groan of a Martyr's woe
Is an Arrow from the Almightie's Bow.

THE SEVEN EYES OF GOD SAID

"Let the Human Organs be kept in their perfect Integrity,
"At will Contracting into Worms or Expanding into Gods,
"And then, behold! what are these Ulro Visions of Chastity?

"Then as the moss upon the tree, or dust upon the plow,
"Or as the sweat upon the labouring shoulder, or as the chaff
"Of the wheat-floor, or as the dregs of the sweet wine-press:
"Such are these Ulro Visions; for tho' we sit down within
"The plowed furrow, list'ning to the weeping clods till we
"Contract or Expand Space at will, or if we raise ourselves
"Upon the chariots of the morning, Contracting or Expanding
        Time,
"Every one knows we are One Family, One Man blessed for ever."

THE DAUGHTERS OF ALBION REPLY

"What may Man be? who can tell! But what may Women be
"To have power over Man from Cradle to corruptible Grave?
"He who is an Infant and whose Cradle is a Manger
"Knoweth the Infant sorrow, whence it came and where it goeth
"And who weave it a Cradle of the grass that withereth away.
"This World is all a Cradle for the erred wandering Phantom,
"Rock'd by Year, Month, Day & Hour; and every two Moments
"Between dwells a Daughter of Beulah to feed the Human
       Vegetable.
"Etune, Daughters of Albion, your hymning Chorus mildly,
"Cord of affection thrilling extatic on the iron Reel
"To the golden Loom of Love, to the moth-labour'd Woof,
"A Garment and Cradle weaving for the infantine Terror,
"For fear, at entering the gate into our World of cruel
"Lamentation, it flee back & hide in Non-Entity's dark wild
"Where dwells the Spectre of Albion, destroyer of Definite Form.
"The Sun shall be a Scythed Chariot of Britain: the Moon, a Ship
"In the British Ocean, Created by Los's Hammer, measured out
"Into Days & Nights & Years & Months, to travel with my feet
"Over these desolate rocks of Albion. O daughters of despair!
"Rock the Cradle, and in mild melodies tell me where found
"What you have enwoven with so much tears & care, so much
"Tender artifice, to laugh, to weep, to learn, to know:
"Remember! recollect! what dark befel in wintry days."

CATHEDRON'S LOOMS

And in the North Gate, in the West of the North, toward Beulah,
Cathedron's Looms are builded, and Los's Furnaces in the South.
A wondrous golden Building immense with ornaments sublime
Is bright Cathedron's golden Hall, its Courts, Towers &
       Pinnacles.

And one Daughter of Los sat at the fiery Reel, & another
Sat at the shining Loom with her Sisters attending round,

Terrible their distress, & their sorrow cannot be utter'd;
And another Daughter of Los sat at the Spining Wheel,
Endless their labour, with bitter food, void of sleep;
Tho' hungry, they labour: they rouze themselves anxious
Hour after hour labouring at the whirling Wheel,
Many Wheels & as many lovely Daughters sit weeping.
Yet the intoxicating delight that they take in their work
Obliterates every other evil; none pities their tears,
Yet they regard not pity & they expect no one to pity,
For they labour for life & love regardless of any one
But the poor Spectres that they work for always, incessantly.

They are mock'd by every one that passes by; they regard not,
They labour, & when their Wheels are broken by scorn & malice
They mend them sorrowing with many tears & afflictions.

Other Daughters Weave on the Cushion & Pillow Network fine
That Rahab & Tirzah may exist & live & breathe & love.
Ah, that it could be as the Daughters of Beulah wish!

Other Daughters of Los, labouring at Looms less fine,
Create the Silk-worm & the Spider & the Catterpiller
To assist in their most grievous work of pity & compassion;
And others Create the wooly Lamb & the downy Fowl
To assist in the work; the Lamb bleats, the Sea-fowl cries;
Men understand not the distress & the labour & sorrow
That in the Interior Worlds is carried on in fear & trembling,
Weaving the shudd'ring fears & loves of Albion's Families.
Thunderous rage the Spindles of iron, & the iron Distaff
Maddens in the fury of their hands, weaving in bitter tears
The veil of Goats-hair & Purple & Scarlet & fine twined Linen.

For the Male is a Furnace of beryll, the Female is a golden Loom.

125

THE DIVINE VOICE *replied:*

"Behold, in the Visions of Elohim Jehovah, behold Joseph & Mary
"And be comforted, O Jerusalem, in the Visions of Jehovah
    Elohim."

She looked & saw Joseph the Carpenter in Nazareth & Mary
His espoused Wife. And Mary said, "If thou put me away from thee
"Dost thou not murder me?" Joseph spoke in anger & fury,
    "Should I
"Marry a Harlot & an Adulteress?" Mary answer'd, "Art thou
    more pure
"Than thy Maker who forgiveth Sins & calls again Her that is Lost?
"Tho' She hates, he calls her again in love. I love my dear Joseph,
"But he driveth me away from his presence; yet I hear the voice of
    God
"In the voice of my Husband : tho' he is angry for a moment, he
    will not
"Utterly cast me away; if I were pure, never could I taste the sweets
"Of the Forgiveness of Sins; if I were holy, I never could behold
    the tears
"Of love, of him who loves me in the midst of his anger in furnace
    of fire."

"Ah my Mary !" said Joseph, weeping over & embracing her
    closely in
His arms : "Doth he forgive Jerusalem, & not exact Purity from
    her who is
"Polluted? I heard his voice in my sleep & his Angel in my dream,
"Saying, 'Doth Jehovah Forgive a Debt only on condition that it
    shall
" 'Be Payed? Doth he Forgive Pollution only on conditions of
    Purity?
" 'That Debt is not Forgiven ! That Pollution is not Forgiven !
" 'Such is the Forgiveness of the Gods, the Moral Virtues of the
" 'Heathen whose tender Mercies are Cruelty. But Jehovah's
    Salvation
" 'Is without Money & without Price, in the Continual Forgiveness
    of Sins,

" 'In the Perpetual Mutual Sacrifice in Great Eternity; for behold,
" 'There is none that liveth & Sinneth not! And this is the Covenant
" 'Of Jehovah: If you Forgive one-another, so shall Jehovah
        Forgive You,
" 'That He Himself may Dwell among you. Fear not then to take
" 'To thee Mary thy Wife, for she is with Child by the Holy Ghost.' "

Then Mary burst forth into a Song: she flowed like a river of
Many Streams in the arms of Joseph & gave forth her tears of joy
Like many waters, and Emanating into gardens & palaces upon
Euphrates, & to forests & floods & animals wild & tame from
Gihon to Hiddekel, & to corn fields & villages & inhabitants
Upon Pison & Arnon & Jordan. And I heard the voice among
The Reapers, Saying, "Am I Jerusalem the lost Adulteress? or am I
"Babylon come up to Jerusalem?" And another voice answer'd,
        Saying,

"Does the voice of my Lord call me again? am I pure thro' his Mercy
"And Pity? Am I become lovely as a Virgin in his sight, who am
"Indeed a Harlot drunken with the Sacrifice of Idols? does he
"Call her pure as he did in the days of her Infancy when She
"Was cast out to the loathing of her person? The Chaldean took
"Me from my Cradle. The Amalekite stole me away upon his
        Camels
"Before I had ever beheld with love the Face of Jehovah, or known
"That there was a God of Mercy. O Mercy, O Divine Humanity!
"O Forgiveness & Pity & Compassion! If I were Pure I should
        never
"Have known Thee: If I were Unpolluted I should never have
"Glorified thy Holiness or rejoiced in thy great Salvation."

THEN LEFT THE SONS OF URIZEN
THE PLOW

Then left the Sons of Urizen the plow & harrow, the loom,
The hammer & the chisel & the rule & compasses; from London
        fleeing,
They forg'd the sword on Cheviot, the chariot of war & the battle-ax,

The trumpet fitted to mortal battle, & the Flute of summer in
    Annandale;
And all the Arts of Life they chang'd into the Arts of Death in
    Albion.
The hour-glass contemn'd because its simple workmanship
Was like the workmanship of the plowman, & the water wheel
That raises water into cisterns, broken & burn'd with fire
Because its workmanship was like the workmanship of the shepherd;
And in their stead, intricate wheels invented, wheel without wheel,
To perplex youth in their outgoings & to bind to labours in Albion
Of day & night the myriads of eternity: they that may grind
And polish brass & iron hour after hour, laborious task,
Kept ignorant of its use: that they might spend the days of wisdom
In sorrowful drudgery to obtain a scanty pittance of bread,
In ignorance to view a small portion & think that All,
And call it Demonstration, blind to all the simple rules of life.

MAN HAS CLOSED HIMSELF UP . . .

Ah! alas! at the sight of the Victim & at sight of those who are
    smitten,
All who see become what they behold; their eyes are cover'd
With veils of tears and their nostrils & tongues shrunk up,
Their ear bent outwards; as their Victim, so are they, in the pangs
Of unconquerable fear amidst delights of revenge Earth-shaking.
And as their eye & ear shrunk, the heavens shrunk away:
The Divine Vision became First a burning flame, then a column
Of fire, then an awful fiery wheel surrounding earth & heaven,
And then a globe of blood wandering distant in an unknown night.
Afar into the unknown night the mountains fled away,
Six months of mortality, a summer, and six months of mortality, a
    winter.
The Human form began to be alter'd by the Daughters of Albion
And the perceptions to be dissipated into the Indefinite, Becoming
A mighty Polypus nam'd Albion's Tree; they tie the Veins
And Nerves into two knots & the Seed into a double knot.
They look forth; the Sun is shrunk: the Heavens are shrunk

Away into the far remote, and the Trees & Mountains wither'd
Into indefinite cloudy shadows in darkness & separation.
By invisible Hatreds adjoin'd, they seem remote and separate
From each other, and yet are a Mighty Polypus in the Deep!
As the Mistletoe grows on the Oak, so Albion's Tree on Eternity. Lo!
He who will not comingle in Love must be adjoin'd by Hate.

They look forth from Stone-henge: from the Cove round London
    Stone
They look on one another: the mountain calls out to the mountain.
Plinlimmon shrunk away: Snowdon trembled: the mountains
Of Wales & Scotland beheld the descending War, the routed flying.
Red run the streams of Albion: Thames is drunk with blood
As Gwendolen cast the shuttle of war, as Cambel return'd the beam,
The Humber & the Severn are drunk with the blood of the slain.
London feels his brain cut round: Edinburgh's heart is
    circumscribed:
York & Lincoln hide among the flocks because of the griding Knife.
Worcester & Hereford, Oxford & Cambridge reel & stagger
Overwearied with howling. Wales & Scotland alone sustain the
    fight!
The inhabitants are sick to death: they labour to divide into Days
And Nights the uncertain Periods, and into Weeks & Months. In
    Vain
They send the Dove & Raven in vain the Serpent over the
    mountains
And in vain the Eagle & Lion over the four-fold wilderness:
They return not, but generate in rocky places desolate:
They return not, but build a habitation separate from Man.
The Sun forgets his course like a drunken man; he hesitates
Upon the Cheselden hills, thinking to sleep on the Severn.
In vain: he is hurried afar into an unknown Night:
He bleeds in torrents of blood as he rolls thro' heaven above.
He chokes up the paths of the sky; the Moon is leprous as snow,
Trembling & descending down, seeking to rest on high Mona,
Scattering her leprous snows in flakes of disease over Albion.
The Stars flee remote; the heaven is iron, the earth is sulphur,
And all the mountains & hills shrink up like a withering gourd

As the Senses of Men shrink together under the Knife of flint
In the hands of Albion's Daughters among the Druid Temples ...

WHAT IS ABOVE IS WITHIN

What is Above is Within, for every-thing in Eternity is translucent:
The Circumference is Within, Without is formed the Selfish Center,
And the Circumference still expands going forward to Eternity,
And the Center has Eternal States; these States we now explore.

And these the Names of Albion's Twelve Sons & of his Twelve
    Daughters
With their Districts: Hand dwelt in Selsey & had Sussex & Surrey
And Kent & Middlesex, all their Rivers & their Hills of flocks &
    herds,
Their Villages, Towns, Cities, Sea-Ports, Temples, sublime
    Catherdrals,
All were his Friends, & their Sons & Daughters intermarry in
    Beulah;
For all are Men in Eternity, Rivers, Mountains, Cities, Villages,
All are Human, & when you enter into their Bosoms you walk
In Heavens & Earths, as in your own Bosom you bear your Heaven
And Earth & all you behold; tho' it appears Without, it is Within,
In your Imagination, of which this world of Mortality is but a
    Shadow.

THE VEIL OF VALA

LOS *uttering thus his vojce:*
"Let Cambel and her Sisters sit within the Mundane Shell
"Forming the fluctuating Globe according to their will:
"According as they weave the little embryon nerves & veins,
"The Eye, the little Nostrils & the delicate Tongue, & Ears
"Of labyrinthine intricacy, so shall they fold the World,
"That whatever is seen upon the Mundane Shell, the same
"Be seen upon the Fluctuating Earth woven by the Sisters.
"And sometimes the Earth shall roll in the Abyss & sometimes
"Stand in the Center & sometimes stretch flat in the Expanse,
"According to the will of the lovely Daughters of Albion;

"Sometimes it shall assimilate with mighty Golgonooza,
"Touching its summits, & sometimes divided roll apart.
"As a beautiful Veil, so these Females shall fold & unfold,
"According to their will, the outside surface of the Earth,
"An outside shadowy Surface superadded to the real Surface
"Which is unchangeable for ever & ever. . .

THE UNIVERSAL ATTRIBUTES

Los cries: "No Individual ought to appropriate to Himself
"Or to his Emanation any of the Universal Characteristics
"Of David or of Eve, of the Woman or of the Lord,
"Of Reuben or of Benjamin, of Joseph of Judah or Levi.
"Those who dare appropriate to themselves Universal Attributes
"Are the Blasphemous Selfhoods, & must be broken asunder.
"A Vegetated Christ & a Virgin Eve are the Hermaphroditic
"Blasphemy; by his Maternal Birth he is that Evil-One
"And his Maternal Humanity must be put off Eternally,
"Lest the Sexual Generation swallow up Regeneration.
"Come Lord Jesus, take on thee the Satanic Body of Holiness!"

THE WORSHIP OF GOD

"It is easier to forgive an Enemy than to forgive a Friend.
"The man who permits you to injure him deserves your vengence:
"He also will receive it; go Spectre! obey my most secret desire
"Which thou knowest without my speaking. Go to these Fiends
    of Righteousness,
"Tell them to obey their Humanities & not pretend Holiness
"When they are murderers: as far as my Hammer & Anvil permit.
"Go, tell them that the Worship of God is honouring his gifts
"In other men: & loving the greatest men best, each according
"To his Genius: which is the Holy Ghost in Man; there is no
    other
"God than that God who is the intellectual fountain of Humanity.

"He who envies or calumniates, which is murder & cruelty,
"Murders the Holy-one. Go, tell them this, & overthrow their cup,
"Their bread, their altar-table, their incense & their oath,
"Their marriage & their baptism, their burial & consecration.
"I have tried to make friends by corporeal gifts but have only
"Made enemies. I never made friends but by spiritual gifts,
"By severe contentions of friendship & the burning fire of thought.
"He who would see the Divinity must see him in his Children,
"One first, in friendship & love, then a Divine Family, & in the midst
"Jesus will appear; so he who wishes to see a Vision, a perfect Whole,
"Must see it in its Minute Particulars, Organized, & not as thou,
"O Fiend of Righteousness, pretendest; thine is a Disorganized
"And snowy cloud, brooder of tempests & destructive War.
"You smile with pomp & rigor, you talk of benevolence & virtue;
"I act with benevolence & Virtue & get murder'd time after time.
"You accumlate Particulars & murder by analyzing, that you
"May take the aggregate, & you call the aggregate Moral Law,
"And you call that swell'd & bloated Form a Minute Particular;
"But General Forms have their vitality in Particulars, & every
"Particular is a Man, a Divine Member of the Divine Jesus."

So Los cried at his Anvil in the horrible darkness weeping.

The Spectre builded stupendous Works, taking the Starry Heavens
Like to a curtain & folding them according to his will,
Repeating the Smaragdine Table of Hermes to draw Los down
Into the Indefinite, refusing to believe without demonstration.
Los reads the Stars of Albion, the Spectre reads the Voids
Between the Stars among the arches of Albion's Tomb sublime,
Rolling the Sea in rocky paths, forming Leviathan
And Behemoth, the War by Sea enormous & the War
By Land astounding, erecting pillars in the deepest Hell
To reach the heavenly arches. Los beheld undaunted, furious,
His heav'd Hammer; he swung it round & at one blow
In unpitying ruin driving down the pyramids of pride,
Smiting the Spectre on his Anvil & the integuments of his Eye
And Ear unbinding in dire pain, with many blows
Of strict severity self-subduing, & with many tears labouring.

Then he sent forth the Spectre: all his pyramids were grains
Of sand, & his pillars dust on the fly's wing, & his starry
Heavens a moth of gold & silver, mocking his anxious grasp.
Thus Los alter'd his Spectre, & every Ratio of his Reason
He alter'd time after time with dire pain & many tears
Till he had completely divided him into a separate space.

Terrified Los sat to behold, trembling & weeping & howling:
"I care not whether a Man is Good or Evil; all that I care
"Is whether he is a Wise Man or a Fool. Go, put off Holiness
"And put on Intellect, or my thund'rous Hammer shall drive thee
"To wrath which thou condemnest, till thou obey my voice."

The Everlasting Gospel

I

If Moral Virtue was Christianity,
Christ's Pretensions were all Vanity,
And Caiphas & Pilate, Men
Praise Worthy, & the Lion's Den
And not the Sheepfold, Allegories
Of God & Heaven & their Glories.
The Moral Christian is the Cause
Of the Unbeliever & his Laws.
The Roman Virtues, Warlike Fame,
Take Jesus' & Jehovah's Name;
For what is Antichrist but those
Who against Sinners Heaven close
With Iron bars, in Virtuous State,
And Rhadamanthus at the Gate?

2

What can this Gospel of Jesus be?
What Life & Immortality,
What was it that he brought to Light
That Plato & Cicero did not write?

The Heathen Deities wrote them all,
These Moral Virtues, great & small.
What is the Accusation of Sin
But Moral Virtues' deadly Gin?
The Moral Virtues in their Pride
Did o'er the World triumphant ride
In Wars & Sacrifice for Sin,
And Souls to Hell ran trooping in.
The Accuser, Holy God of All
This Pharisaic Worldly Ball,
Amidst them in his Glory Beams
Upon the Rivers & the Streams.
Then Jesus rose & said to Me,
"Thy Sins are all forgiven thee."
Loud Pilate Howl'd, loud Caiphas yell'd,
When they the Gospel Light beheld.
It was when Jesus said to Me,
"Thy Sins are all forgiven thee."
The Christian trumpets loud proclaim
Thro' all the World in Jesus' name
Mutual forgiveness of each Vice,
And oped the Gates of Paradise.
The Moral Virtues in Great fear
Formed the Cross & Nails & Spear,
And the Accuser standing by
Cried out, "Crucify! Crucify!
"Our Moral Virtues ne'er can be,
"Nor Warlike pomp & Majesty;
"For Moral Virtues all begin
"In the Accusations of Sin,
"And all the Heroic Virtues End
"In destroying the Sinner's Friend.
"Am I not Lucifer the Great,
"And you my daughters in Great State,
"The fruit of my Mysterious Tree
"Of Good & Evil & Misery
"And Death & Hell, which now begin
"On everyone who Forgives Sin?"

a

The Vision of Christ that thou dost see
Is my Vision's Greatest Enemy:
Thine has a great hook nose like thine,
Mine has a snub nose like to mine:
Thine is the friend of All Mankind,
Mine speaks in parables to the Blind:
Thine loves the same world that mine hates,
Thy Heaven doors are my Hell Gates.
Socrates taught what Meletus
Loath'd as a Nation's bitterest Curse,
And Caiphas was in his own Mind
A benefactor to Mankind:
Both read the Bible day & night,
But thou read'st black where I read white.

b

Was Jesus gentle, or did he
Give any marks of Gentility?
When twelve years old he ran away
And left his Parents in dismay.
When after three days' sorrow Found,
Loud as Sinai's trumpet sound:
"No Earthly Parents I confess—
"My Heavenly Father's business!
"Ye understand not what I say,
"And, angry, force me to obey."
Obedience is a duty then,
And favour gains with God & Men.
John from the Wilderness loud cried;
Satan gloried in his Pride.

"Come," said Satan, "come away,
"I'll soon see if you'll obey!
"John for disobedience bled,
"But you can turn the stones to bread.
"God's high king & God's high Priest
"Shall Plant their Glories in your breast

"If Caiaphas you will obey,
"If Herod you with bloody Prey
"Feed with the sacrifice, & be
"Obedient, fall down, worship me."
Thunders & lightnings broke around,
And Jesus' voice in thunders' sound:
"Thus I seize the Spiritual Prey.
"Ye smiters with disease, make way.
"I come your King & God to seize.
"Is God a smiter with disease?"
The God of this World raged in vain:
He bound Old Satan in his Chain,
And bursting forth his furious ire
Became a Chariot of fire.
Throughout the land he took his course,
And traced diseases to their source:
He curs'd the Scribe & Pharisee,
Trampling down Hipocrisy:
Where'er his Chariot took its way,
There Gates of death let in the day,
Broke down from every Chain & Bar;
And Satan in his Spiritual War
Drag'd at his Chariot wheels: loud howl'd
The God of this World: louder roll'd
The Chariot Wheels, & louder still
His voice was heard from Zion's hill,
And in his hand the Scourge shone bright;
He scourg'd the Merchant Canaanite
From out the Temple of his Mind,
And in his Body tight does bind
Satan & all his Hellish Crew;
And thus with wrath he did subdue
The Serpent Bulk of Nature's dross,
Till He had nail'd it to the Cross.
He took on Sin in the Virgin's Womb,
And put it off on the Cross & Tomb
To be Worship'd by the Church of Rome.

Was Jesus Humble? or did he
Give any Proofs of Humility?
Boast of high Things with Humble tone,
And give with Charity a Stone?
When but a Child he ran away
And left his Parents in dismay.
When they had wander'd three days long
These were the words upon his tongue:
"No Earthly Parents I confess:
"I am doing my Father's business."
When the rich learned Pharisee
Came to consult him secretly,
Upon his heart with Iron pen
He wrote, "Ye must be born again."
He was too proud to take a bride;
He spoke with authority, not like a Scribe.
He says with most consummate Art,
"Follow me, I am meek & lowly of heart,"
As that is the only way to escape
The Miser's net & the Glutton's trap.
What can be done with such desperate Fools
Who follow after the Heathen Schools?
I was standing by when Jesus died;
What I call'd Humility, they call'd Pride.
He who loves his Enemies betrays his Friends;
This surely is not what Jesus intends,
But the sneaking Pride of Heroic Schools,
And the Scribes' & Pharisees' Virtuous Rules;
For he acts with honest, triumphant Pride,
And this is the cause that Jesus died.
He did not die with Christian Ease,
Asking pardon of his Enemies:
If he had, Caiaphas would forgive;
Sneaking submission can always live.
He had only to say that God was the devil,

And the devil was God, like a Christian Civil:
Mild Christian regrets to the devil confess
For affronting him thrice in the Wilderness;
Like dr. Priestly & Bacon & Newton—
He had soon been bloody Caesar's Elf,
And at last he would have been Caesar himself.
Poor Spiritual Knowledge is not worth a button!
For thus the Gospel Sir Isaac confutes:
"God can only be known by his Attributes;
"And as for the Indwelling of the Holy Ghost
"Or of Christ & his Father, it's all a boast
"And Pride & Vanity if the imagination,
"That disdains to follow this World's Fashion."
To teach doubt & Experiment
Certainly was not what Christ meant.
What was he doing all that time,
From twelve years old to manly prime?
Was he then Idle, or the Less
About his Father's business?
Or was his wisdom held in scorn
Before his wrath began to burn
In Miracles throughout the land,
That quite unnerv'd Caiaphas' hand?
If he had been Antichrist, Creeping Jesus,
He'd have done any thing to please us—
Gone sneaking into Synagogues
And not us'd the Elders & Priests like dogs,
But Humble as a Lamb or Ass
Obey'd himself to Caiaphas.
God wants not Man to Humble himself:
This is the trick of the ancient Elf.
This is the Race that Jesus ran:
Humble to God, Haughty to Man,
Cursing the Rulers before the People
Even to the temple's highest Steeple;
And when he Humbled himself to God,
Then descended the Cruel Rod.
"If thou humblest thyself, thou humblest me;

"Thou also dwell'st in Eternity.
"Thou art a Man, God is no more,
"Thy own humanity learn to adore,
"For that is my Spirit of Life.
"Awake, arise to Spiritual Strife
"And thy Revenge abroad display
"In terrors at the Last Judgment day.
"God's Mercy & Long Suffering
"Is but the Sinner to Judgment to bring.
"Thou on the Cross for them shalt pray
"And take Revenge at the last Day.
Jesus replied & thunders hurl'd:
"I never will Pray for the World.
"Once I did so when I pray'd in the Garden;
"I wish'd to take with me a Bodily Pardon."
Can that which was of woman born
In the absence of the Morn,
When the Soul fell into Sleep
And Archangels round it weep,
Shooting out against the Light
Fibres of a deadly night,
Reasoning upon its own dark Fiction,
In doubt which is Self Contradiction?
Humility is only doubt,
And does the Sun & Moon blot out,
Rooting over with thorns & stems
The buried Soul & all its Gems.
This Life's dim Windows of the Soul
Distorts the Heavens from Pole to Pole
And leads you to believe a Lie
When you see with, not thro', the Eye
That was born in a night to perish in a night,
When the Soul slept in the beams of Light.
Was Jesus Chaste? or did he, &ᶜ

e

Was Jesus Chaste? or did he
Give any Lessons of Chastity?

The morning blush'd fiery red:
Mary was found in Adulterous bed;
Earth groan'd beneath, & Heaven above
Trembled at discovery of Love.
Jesus was sitting in Moses' Chair,
They brought the trembling Woman There.
Moses commands she be stoned to death,
What was the sound of Jesus' breath?
He laid His hands on Moses' Law:
The Ancient Heavens, in Silent Awe
Writ with Curses from Pole to Pole,
All away began to roll:
The Earth trembling & Naked lay
In secret bed of Mortal Clay,
On Sinai felt the hand divine
Putting back the bloody shrine,
And she heard the breath of God
As she heard by Eden's flood:
"Good & Evil are no more!
"Sinai's trumpets, cease to roar!
"Cease, finger of God, to write!
"The Heavens are not clean in thy Sight.
"Thou art Good, & thou Alone;
"Nor may the sinner cast one stone.
"To be Good only, is to be
"A God or else a Pharisee.
"Thou Angel of the Presence Divine
"That didst create this Body of Mine,
"Wherefore has thou writ these Laws
"And Created Hell's dark jaws?
"My Presence I will take from thee:
"A Cold Leper thou shalt be.
"Tho' thou wast so pure & bright
"That Heaven was Impure in thy Sight,
"Tho' thy Oath turn'd Heaven Pale,
"Tho' thy Covenant built Hell's Jail,
"Tho' thou didst all to Chaos roll
"With the Serpent for its soul,

140

"Still the breath Divine does move
"And the breath Divine is Love
"Mary, Fear Not! Let me see
"The Seven Devils that torment thee:
"Hide not from my Sight thy Sin,
"That forgiveness thou maist win.
"Has no Man Condemned thee?"
"No Man, Lord:" " then what is he
"Who shall Accuse thee? Come Ye forth,
"Fallen fiends of Heav'nly birth
"That have forgot your Ancient love
"And driven away my trembling Dove.
"You shall bow before her feet;
"You shall lick the dust for Meat;
"And tho' you cannot Love, but Hate,
"Shall be beggars at Love's Gate.
"What was thy love? Let me see it;
"Was it love or Dark Deceit?"
"Love too long from Me has fled;
" 'Twas dark deceit, to Earn my bread;
" 'Twas Covet, or 'twas Custom or
"Some trifle not worth caring for;
"That they may call a shame & Sin
"Love's temple that God dwelleth in
"And hide in secret hidden Shrine
"The Naked Human form divine,
"And render that a Lawless thing
"On which the Soul Expands its wing.
"But this, O Lord, this was my Sin
"When first I let these Devils in
"In dark pretence to Chastity:
"Blaspheming Love, blaspheming thee.
"Thence Rose Secret Adulteries,
"And thence did Covet also rise.
"My sin thou hast forgiven me,
"Canst thou forgive my Blasphemy?
"Canst thou return to this dark Hell,
"And in my burning bosom dwell?

"And canst thou die that I may live?
"And canst thou Pity & forgive?"
Then Roll'd the shadowy Man away
From the Limbs of Jesus, to make them his prey,
An Ever devouring appetite
Glittering with festering Venoms bright,
Crying, "Crucify this cause of distress,
"Who don't keep the secrets of Holiness!
"All Mental Powers by Diseases we bind,
"But he heals the deaf & the Dumb & the Blind.
"Whom God has afflicted for Secret Ends,
"He comforts & Heals & calls them Friends."
But, when Jesus was Crucified,
Then was perfected his glitt'ring pride:
In three Nights he devour'd his prey,
And still he devours the Body of Clay;
For dust & Clay is the Serpent's meat,
Which never was made for Man to Eat.

f

I am sure This Jesus will not do
Either for Englishman or Jew.
Did Jesus teach doubt? or did he
Give any lessons of Philosophy,
Charge Visionaries with decieving,
Or call Men wise for not Believing?

i

Was Jesus Born of a Virgin Pure
With narrow Soul & looks demure?
If he intended to take on Sin
The Mother should an Harlot been,
Just such a one as Magdalen
With seven devils in her Pen;
Or were Jew Virgins still more Curst,
And more sucking devils nurst?
Or what was it which he took on
That he might bring Salvation?

A Body subject to be Tempted,
From neither pain nor grief Exempted?
Or such a body as might not feel
The passions that with Sinners deal?
Yes, but they say he never fell.
Ask Caiaphas; for he can tell.
"He mock'd the Sabbath, & he mock'd
"The Sabbath's God, & he unlock'd
"The Evil spirits from their Shrines,
"And turn'd Fishermen to Divines;
"O'erturn'd the Tent of Secret Sins,
"& its Golden cords & Pins—
" 'Tis the Bloody Shrine of War
"Pinn'd around from Star to Star,
"Halls of justice, hating Vice,
"Where the devil Combs his lice.
"He turn'd the devils into Swine
"That he might tempt the Jews to dine;
"Since which, a Pig has got a look
"That for a Jew may be mistook.
" 'Obey your parents.'—What says he?
" 'Woman, what have I to do with thee?
" 'No Earthly Parents I confess:
" 'I am doing my Father's Business.'
"He scorn'd Earth's Parents, scorn'd Earth's God,
"And mock'd the one & the other's Rod;
"His Seventy Disciples sent
"Against Religion & Government:
"They by the Sword of Justice fell
"And him their Cruel Murderer tell.
"He left his Father's trade to roam
"A wand'ring Vagrant without Home;
"And thus he others' labour stole
"That he might live above Controll.
"The Publicans & Harlots he
"Selected for his Company,
"And from the Adultress turn'd away
"God's righteous Law, that lost its Prey."

For the Sexes:
The Gates of Paradise

[FRONTISPIECE]

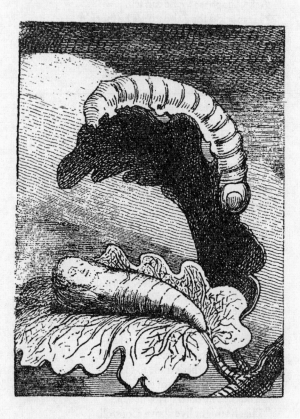

WHAT IS MAN?

The Sun's Light when he unfolds it
Depends on the Organ that beholds it.

[PROLOGUE]

Mutual Forgiveness of each Vice,
Such are the Gates of Paradise.
Against the Accuser's chief desire,
Who walk'd among the Stones of Fire,
Jehovah's Finger Wrote the Law:
Then Wept! then rose in Zeal & Awe,
And in the midst of Sinai's heat
Hid it beneath his Mercy Seat.
And the Dead Corpse from Sinai's heat
Buried beneath his Mercy Seat.
O Christians, Christians! tell me Why
You rear it on your Altars high.

THE KEYS

The Catterpiller on the Leaf
Reminds thee of thy Mother's Grief.

OF THE GATES

My Eternal Man set in Repose,
The Female from his darkness rose
And She found me beneath a Tree,
A Mandrake, & in her Veil hid me.
Serpent Reasonings us entice
Of Good & Evil, Virtue & Vice.
Doubt Self Jealous, Wat'ry folly,
Struggling thro' Earth's Melancholy.
Naked in Air, in Shame & Fear,
Blind in Fire with shield & spear,
Two Horn'd Reasoning Cloven Fiction,

In Doubt, which is Self contradiction,
A dark Hermaphrodite I stood,
Rational Truth, Root of Evil & Good.
Round me flew the Flaming Sword;
Round her snowy Whirlwinds roar'd,
Freezing her Veil, the Mundane Shell.
I rent the Veil where the Dead dwell:

When weary Man enters his Cave
He meets his Saviour in the Grave
Some find a Female Garment there,
And some a Male, woven with care,
Lest the Sexual Garments sweet
Should grow a devouring Winding sheet,
One Dies! Alas! the Living & Dead,
One is slain & One is fled.
In Vain-glory hatch & nurst,
By double Spectres Self Accurst,
My Son! my Son! thou treatest me
But as I have instructed thee.
On the shadows of the Moon
Climbing thro' Night's highest noon.
In Time's Ocean falling drown'd.
In Aged Ignorance profound,
Holy & cold, I clip'd the Wings
Of all Sublunary Things,
And in depths of my Dungeons
Closed the Father & the Sons.
But when once I did descry
The Immortal Man that cannot Die,
Thro' evening shades I haste away
To close the Labours of my Day.
The Door of Death I open found
And the Worm Weaving in the Ground:
Thou'rt my Mother from the Womb,
Wife, Sister, Daughter, to the Tomb,
Weaving to Dreams the Sexual strife
And weeping over the Web of Life.

[EPILOGUE]

To The Accuser who is
The God of This World

Truly, My Satan, thou art but a Dunce,
And dost not know the Garment from the Man.
Every Harlot was a Virgin once,
Nor can'st thou ever change Kate into Nan.

Tho' thou art Worship'd by the Names Divine
Of Jesus & Jehovah, thou art still
The Son of Morn in weary Night's decline,
The lost Traveller's Dream under the Hill.

Index of First Lines